T Designs
Tara Elizabeth Brittingham
1440 Michelline Court
Hoffman Estates, IL 60195

T Designs
Tara Elizabeth Brittingham

PACKAGE
design &
BRAND
identity

COLEMAN, LIPUMA, SEGAL & MORRILL, INC.

38 Case Studies of Strategic Imagery for the Marketplace

First published in the United States of America by:
Rockport Publishers, Inc.
146 Granite Street
Rockport, Massachusetts 01966
Telephone: (508) 546-9590
Fax: (508) 546-7141
Telex: 5106019284 ROCKORT PUB

Distributed to the book trade and art trade in the U.S. and
Canada by:
North Light, an imprint of
F & W Publications
1507 Dana Avenue
Cincinnati, Ohio 45207
Telephone: (513) 531-2222

Other Distribution by:
Rockport Publishers, Inc.
Rockport, Massachusetts 01966

ISBN 1-56496-041-2

10 9 8 7 6 5 4 3 2 1

Package Design Concepts:
Coleman, LiPuma, Segal & Morrill, Inc.
Editor: Joyce Forrester, CLS&M
Product Photography and Office Interiors:
Michael Anthony Studio
Production Manager: Barbara States
Layout/Mechanicals: Sara Day Studio
Printed in Singapore

PACKAGE
design &
BRAND
identity

COLEMAN, LIPUMA, SEGAL & MORRILL, INC.

38 Case Studies of Strategic Imagery for the Marketplace

ROCKPORT

ROCKPORT PUBLISHERS · ROCKPORT, MASSACHUSETTS

CLS&M CONTENTS

Shopping can be a remarkably intense experience. Even if you merely stop by the market to pick up a quart of milk or laundry detergent, you pass aisles and aisles of brightly colored boxes, jars, cans, tubes, and cartons. In these brief five seconds of your shopping experience, the packaging becomes the ultimate selling vehicle. The package is the message. The package is the product you will ultimately select or perhaps ignore and pass by. When shoppers think about products, they don't think of the color in the Jack Daniel's bottle, they don't think of the applesauce inside the Gerber Baby Food jar, they don't think of the powder in an Arm & Hammer package. Close your eyes and visualize Coca-Cola, Tide, and Campbell Soup. The first things that come to mind are the colors and the symbols on the packaging. The package is what grabs the shopper's attention, and within those precious five seconds the package has to communicate a wealth of information.

In reality, most shoppers do not decide exactly what to buy until they reach the shelves in their local supermarket. That means that a great deal of advertising is going on in the last five seconds before a sale.

It's no wonder then that manufacturers devote so much attention to the design of packages. The package protects, contains and, perhaps most importantly, promotes a product.

The challenge is to design a package that:
- Instantly grabs the shopper's eye, even when it is shelved alongside hundreds of competing brands.
- Identifies the product.
- Reflects the quality of the product.

The creative challenge to fulfill these criteria of packaging effectiveness can be especially demanding when faced with the proposition of redesigning existing packaging. Experience has shown that packaging change for an established product can pose a significant risk--as well as an opportunity-- if the designer fails to recognize the packaging elements that hold equity for the brand. Whether shape, color, typeface, illustration or other unique graphic element, it is crucial to know, prior to the start of the redesign process, which, if any, of these elements triggers shoppers' recognition of the brand.

As mentioned, from the shopper's point of view, the package is the product. For this reason, even when the redesign is intended to give the brand's package a "new," more contemporary look, the intrinsic brand identifying elements must be retained.

Making a packaging change that delivers effectively in each of the key areas that lead to sale is indeed a tall order for the designer. Consumer research has become a valuable tool at the various stages of the design process. At the start, it provides designers with an understanding of the strengths and limitations of existing packaging and the primary "equity" elements on the packaging. Towards the end of the process, it serves client companies in establishing the extent to which the design objectives have been achieved.

CLS&M "Upfront" packaging equity research is conducted by Perception Research Services (PRS) United States and United Kingdom. "Upfront" is a cost efficient program that helps both brand management and design teams in structuring the design objectives.

It also helps isolate the elements on the current packaging that are contributing to recognition on-shelf and positive brand perceptions -- the elements which must be retained as the redesign process begins.

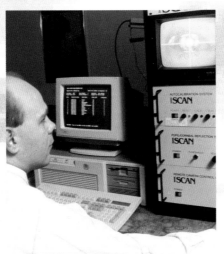

Measuring stopping power
A target shopper seated at
a PRS eye tracker viewing
typical shelf-set image.

Computer instantaneously
displaying and recording
where she's looking.

CLS&M Management & Elliot Young, President of PRS, designed the research procedure to evaluate the overall strength of existing packaging in the key areas of:
- Shelf impact.
- Recall and identification of brand's salient package elements.
- Overall likability.
- Aesthetic appeal of the packaging.
- Effect of the current packaging on brand image.

This CLS&M "Upfront" equity research also quantifies the relative importance of equity elements in generating brand identification and message delivery. Accordingly, the input from brand equity research insures that the design team has the necessary insight at the start of the design process that avoids the risk of franchise loss, and also leads to development of effective packaging and purchase increases.

It's generally acknowledged that in-store impulse purchases account for 65% of the shopper decisions and that the average supermarket now contains more than 20,000 Stock Keeping Units (SKU's). Given this massive clutter, plus the reality that the average shopper is spending only 22 minutes in the supermarket, we come to the realization that 1320 seconds is a brief time period to examine more than 20,000 items. In actuality, approximately one-third of all these items are being totally ignored by the shopper.

In the final five seconds, as the shopper moves through the store, the packaging must "pop" off the shelf, convey valuable information, and entice the shopper to pick up and purchase the product. Deficient packaging can result in another product failure. Effective packaging can insure a product's success.

CLS&M PHILOSOPHY OF DESIGN

Since its founding in 1966, the international marketing communications and design firm Coleman, LiPuma, Segal & Morrill, Inc. (CLS&M) has provided award-winning, innovative and successful design solutions to over 100 corporate clients in the United States and abroad. CLS&M represents a unified body of services which includes package design development and corporate, retail and brand identity design.

The firm supports its creative experience and expertise with a strong marketing component. Its management team includes senior marketing professionals with over 30 years of experience in both product and image marketing in the United States and Europe. The blending of both creative and marketing talents insures that clients receive creative solutions based on a firm strategic marketing foundation.

Understanding the marketing dynamics is the first step in a successful development process. We work with clients to accurately define project problems, opportunities and objectives, to conduct CLS&M "Upfront" pre-design evaluative research, and to audit the competitive retail environment. A thorough knowledge of the retail setting is a key factor in the success of packaging design.

We were pioneers ten years ago in introducing computer-aided graphic design for packaging. Today, CLS&M continues to introduce new computer-aided methodologies into the design process, but we haven't lost sight of the fact that the creative process starts in the mind and on the drawing board. This process allows us to integrate superior design done by hand-- or marker, or pen, or brush--with that done by

Ed Morrill, Abe Segal, Sal LiPuma, Owen W. Coleman
Founders and partners of CLS&M (left to right).

Richard C. Roth
Vice President
Marketing/Sales

Karen Corell
Vice President
Creative Director

computer. The choice of traditional or computer methodology is made based on the needs of each project and each client.

Every project can become fully computerized before it reaches the refinement stage. High-end Macintosh equipment, linked to a high resolution, color-accurate Fiery printer, is used to develop each design to its fullest communication potential.

The computer systems also provide a very important marketing/creative capability--the ability to view the new design concepts (even in the early stages) in a simulated planogram of competitive products at point of purchase. By studying proposed designs in the context of competitve packages in a near-real environment, we can select and fine-tune those designs that maximize shelf impact.

Our firm has also been a part of the great changes in the client approval process. Some clients have had remote viewing systems installed at their offices matched by comparable systems in our offices. The clients can view full-color packaging designs transmitted over telephone lines to give their approval, or to make annotations directly on the screen in "real time" to expedite refinements.

Direct involvement by senior management, a strong foundation in solid marketing principles, a reputation for fresh creativity, our leadership in pioneering the use of computers in graphic design and our flexibility to match our variety of talents to each different client's challenges are the hallmarks of CLS&M's brand design philosophy.

Joyce Forrester
Director of Public
Relations

Steve Merry
Managing Partner
CLS&M Europe

SWEET SUCCESS WEIGHT LOSS PLAN
Nestlé USA, Inc.

Nestlé, a company whose name is synonymous with chocolate, created a new diet product designed especially for chocolate lovers and named it Nestlé Sweet Success. Part of a weight loss program which includes luscious easy-to-prepare shakes, low fat snacks and well balanced meals, the product enables dieters to indulge in the rich chocolate taste which has long been forbidden to them.

The development of the Nestlé Sweet Success brand image was greatly facilitated by the use of computer technology. The smooth, multi-color blend in the word "Success" helps communicate the variety of flavors available in the product line.

The logo, which was executed initially at CLS&M on a Mac Quadra computer as a low resolution file, was recreated on Scitex equipment for final reproduction. Owen Coleman and assistant Pat Martin review the final logo execution before sending the Mac disk to the electronic separator, Techtron L.A.

Initial rough concepts explored the combination of contemporary images with the equity of the Nestlé logotype.

All design concepts were extended to a variety of different product forms and package configurations. They were then computer-cloned to provide multiple images and positioned in rough shelf sets alongside competition.
Design and marketing management has the opportunity to more fully evaluate and select the most effective concepts at an early stage of packaging image development.

12

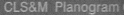

CLS&M Planogram

9.18.91

Historically, the McKesson Water Products Company's major sales were in the home delivery category. With the direction of brand management, marketing/design strategies were established to create and implement a new symbol/trademark that could work across several brand names of long-standing equity for packaging in retail markets.

The final selected design presents a realistic graphic image which does not mislead consumers with snowcapped mountains, streams, etc. This was confirmed in a packaging study conducted by Perception Research Services. The new symbol was positioned over the Sparkletts brand name in the Los Angeles and Texas markets, over the Alhambra brand name in San Francisco and Bay areas and as part of the Crystal brand name in Arizona. In a corporate identity implementation study the new symbol unifies the company and all the individual brands.

Before and after graphics for the Sparkletts brand labels. The final trademark/symbol unifies the different brand names in various markets.

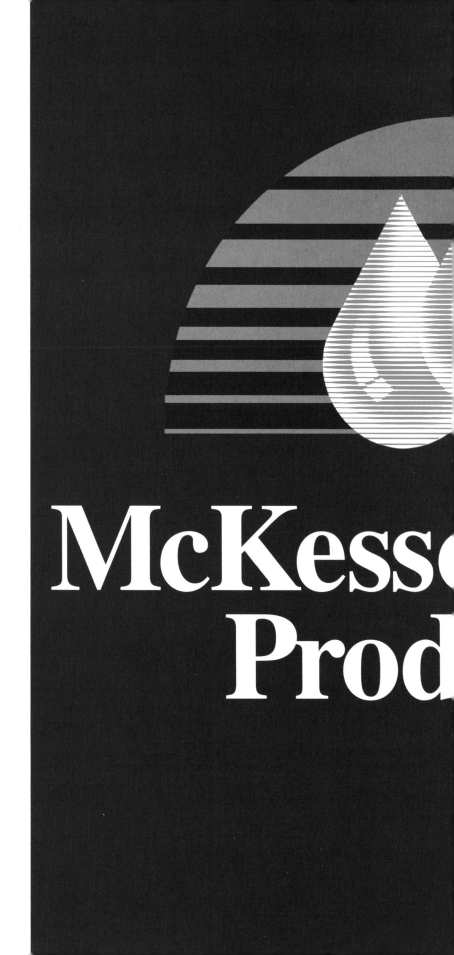

McKesso
Prod

14

Water

cts

Sparkletts®
DRINKING WATER
SODIUM FREE

• Puncture vent hole at top of bottle.
• To pour: Open spout by pressing tab upward.
• To stop: Release tab. Spout will seal automatically.

Alhambra®
DRINKING WATER
SODIUM FREE

McKesson Water
Products Co.
Union City, CA
94587

MINERALS ADDED FOR FLAVOR.
CONTAINS 0 MG. SODIUM PER 8 FL.
OZ. SERVING.

• Twist valve to break seal.
• Pierce hole at top left of bottle.
• Point arrow down and pull valve to pour. Push valve to stop.

GALLONS

Crystal™
DRINKING WATER
SODIUM FREE

McKesson Water
Products Co.
Phoenix, AZ
85017

FROM CRYSTAL'S OWN PROTE
PREPARES D

During an extensive visual audit of McKesson Water Products Company locations, many historical photographs were reviewed. Several of the water brands were established in the 1920's as portrayed on this delivery truck.

The new trademark works well as a one-color graphic representation on the 3.5 gallon home delivery container and the 5 gallon home and office size container.

All labels/graphic concepts were presented to McKesson Water Products Marketing Management in computerized planogram form next to competitive products.

Separate and distinct trademark studies were created and shown as isolated symbols and in context with label graphics.

All new Ortega imagery was executed and positioned as electronic mechanicals for reproduction using Mac Quadra with Adobe Illustrator software and Photoshop for positioning of full-color photography.

In contrast to the blue equity color, another favored design contender of Nabisco Management was the orange to yellow background packaging with the Ortega logo and sun symbol positioned on a strong blue background stamp.

Although this packaging had strong shelf impression in research, the Ortega blue equity color was the overall winner in the research analysis.

Design concept in semi-finished mock-up form.

A broad range of concepts were created initially on the Taco Shell carton and Salsa label. Each design concept was positioned in its own competitive planogram as part of the design presentation phase.

Favored design candidate themes were produced in three-dimensional full-color comprehensive form.

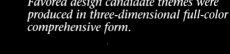

ORTEGA

10

TACO SHELLS

NET WT
1.8 OZ (136g)

ORTEGA

MILD

THICK & CHUNKY

SALSA

Upjohn, manufacturers of Unicap Multi Vitamins, asked Coleman, LiPuma, Segal & Morrill, Inc. to redesign the Unicap packaging. A leader in the field of vitamins since 1940, Upjohn's primary goal was the creation of a new visual imagery that would convey the high standards of the Unicap line. CLS&M developed the graphics, language, photography and package shapes allowing each individual vitamin formula to convey its own uniqueness while simultaneously communicating the strengths of the entire product line.

The existing line of packages was in need of a major graphic and structural upgrade.

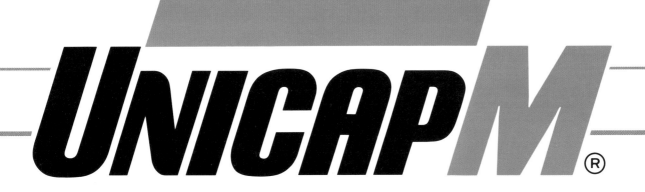

In keeping with the recognizability of Unicap's brand name equity, the new logo-type remains black on white. Contemporary color coding for each formula provides the consumer with a distinctive choice for ease of purchase. The transition toned color band frames the logotype on both the face panel and fifth panel, creating a strong graphic element on store shelf displays. Up-to-date photography, depicting the target audience of each vitamin formula, continues to enhance each product's individual concept, while fresh and concise copy clearly addresses the requirements of the consumer.

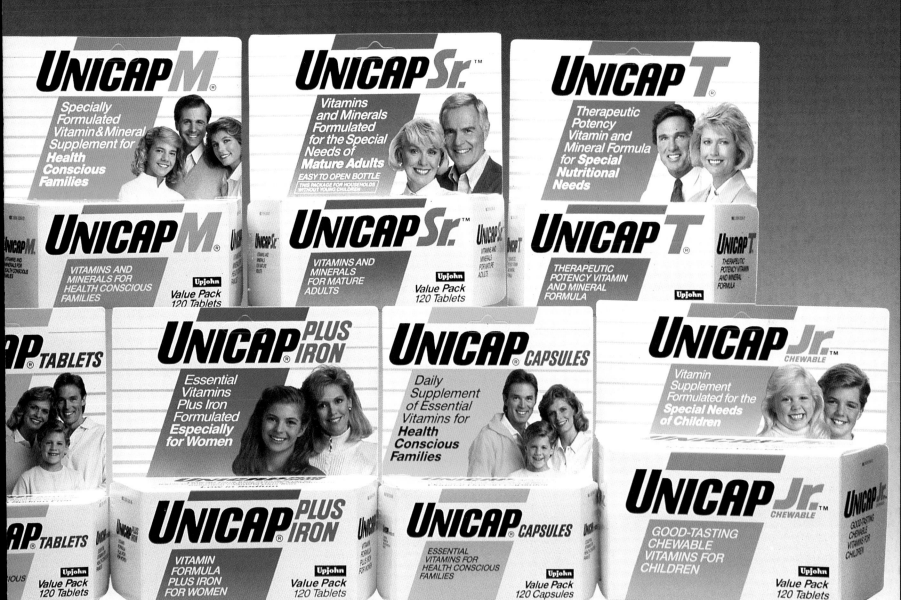

39

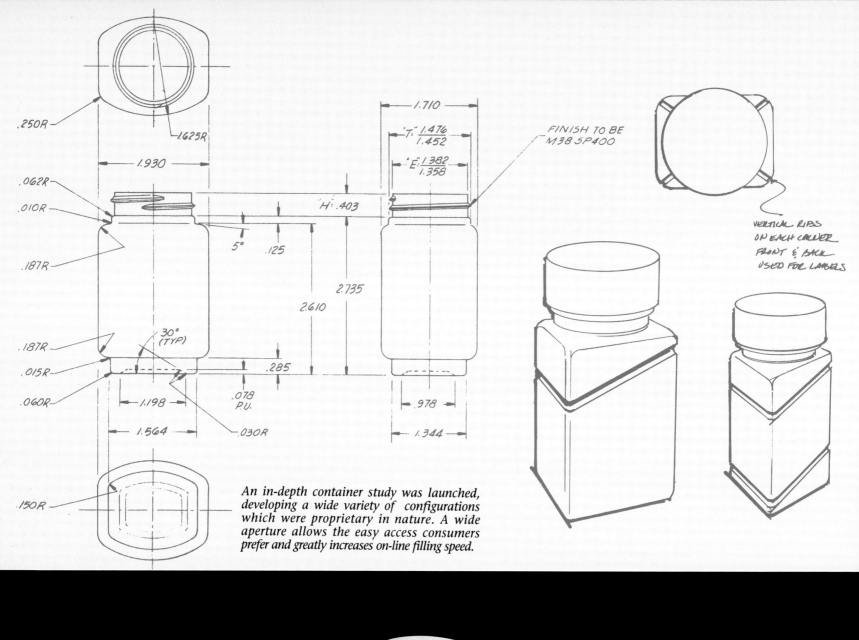

.250R
1.625R
1.930
.062R
.010R
.187R
5°
.125
.187R
30° (TYP)
.015R
.285
.060R
1.198
.078 P.U.
1.564
.030R
.150R

1.710
"T." 1.476 / 1.452
"E." 1.382 / 1.358
H: .403
FINISH TO BE M38 SP400
2.735
2.610
.978
1.344

VERTICAL RIBS ON EACH CORNER FRONT & BACK USED FOR LABELS

An in-depth container study was launched, developing a wide variety of configurations which were proprietary in nature. A wide aperture allows the easy access consumers prefer and greatly increases on-line filling speed.

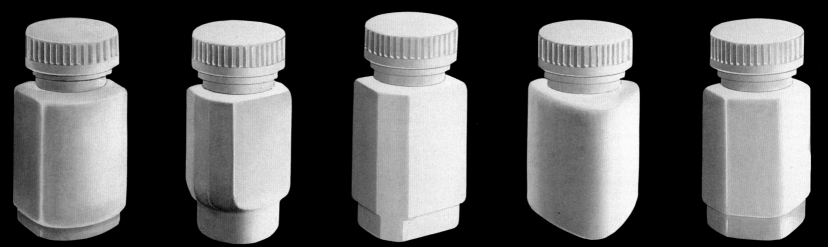

A side-by-side comparison of the old and new imagery conveys the refreshing high quality look that matches the superiority of the product line. The uniquely angled carton, excitingly contemporary in design, presents an eye-catching impression of continuity throughout the line, increasing the highly perceived value of the product. The result is a new, high quality image for Unicap Multi Vitamins and a contemporary look that matches the superiority of the product line. Refreshing, high-tech imagery and carton shape is complemented by the graphic continuity and brand name equity. This image creates a vivid point of purchase impact for the consumer that clearly dominates on-shelf competition. The modern graphics and photography, the concise information and the variety of choices all combine to make Unicap Multi Vitamins a visual standout that guarantees product excellence.

LOGO MOLDED IN ANGLED CORNER INSIDE

OFF-CENTERED CAP FOR EASE OF DISPENSING

The primary container for all Unicap Multi Vitamins, with the exception of Unicap Jr., is made of HDPE plastic for improved efficiency. The curved front and back surfaces, plus the pedestal base, add a contemporary flare of style.

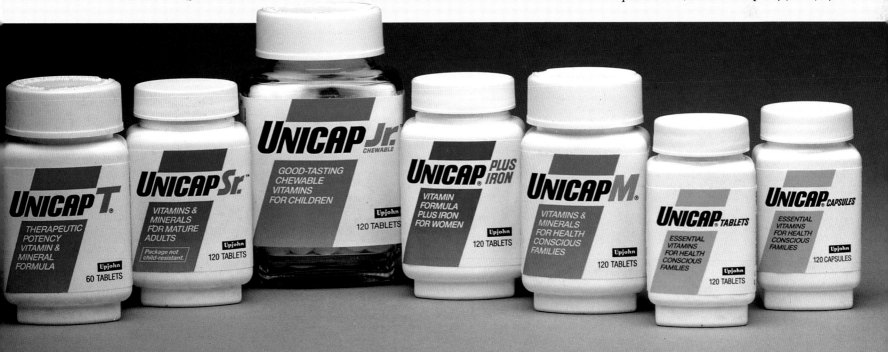

A major redesign of the Aunt Jemima waffle line was created several years ago utilizing CLS&M's Lightspeed computer system. Quaker Oats wanted to retain a strong color code system for each of the products while improving the appetite-appealing photography. Several modest variations were designed. Then the new technology enabled us to view the packaging with a more revolutionary change by maintaining a consistent white background with color-coded borders and typography.

These were probably the first computer planograms to be executed. Although the 35mm slide quality was not critically sharp, it was evident that a strong blocking effect was achieved. Max Lomont, Vice President of Design at Quaker, was so impressed with this new technique that he called in the Divisional President who approved this packaging design in the first phase of creative. Quaker Oats was able to substantially shorten the time frame and beat the competition to shelf with the updated packaging.

Over a period of several years, CLS&M assisted Quaker Marketing in upgrading the trademark portrait of Aunt Jemima.

...ortrait of the original Aunt Jemima ...ademark.

...ightspeed computer-generated planogram of the existing ...unt Jemima waffle line.

The new line image was carried across all Aunt Jemima frozen products.

...ightspeed computer-generated planogram positions a new design format with ...stronger impression for the line next to competitive products.

After several years, new packaging was created with more appetite-appealing photography and implementation of the updated Aunt Jemima trademark.

DEER PARK WATER
Deer Park Spring Water Inc.

The initial criteria established by Deer Park Marketing Management was to retain the equities that had been established in the label design and to design a private mold plastic one gallon size container that would be uniquely associated with the Deer Park brand. Based on the improved sales due to the new container shape, CLS&M designed and prepared a more impactful label design. Critical to the quality attitude of the label was the gradation background from dark to lighter blue. The reverse white logo stood out on shelf next to competitive products. The line expanded to include a 12 fluid ounce size and a 1.5 liter size. These newer container and graphic designs were established to compete with high end water products like Evian. After many years of flat sales, the new design program assisted in a major sales increase.

Before and after private mold container design for a one gallon size.

The graphics were upgraded to achieve more quality and shelf impact next to competitive products.

Deer Park's rolling stock utilized the Deer Park blue color, and the popular advertising phrase was positioned on the top and sides of the truck.

CLS&M designed private mold plastic containers to fit an upscale lifestyle image.

CLS&M developed the corporate identity program for Deer Park including all stationery items, rolling stock, signage and office/home delivery five gallon container graphics.

45

WISH•BONE SALAD DRESSING
Thomas J. Lipton Company

The criteria for the redesign of the regular line of salad dressings called for the creation of a more exciting, distinct and contemporary look to reinforce the quality image of Wish•Bone and reflect a strong family relationship with the line of lite products. The rich "Wish•Bone green" background with a strong, circular shape unifies the line, while the full-bodied salad illustration projects appetite appeal.

A cross-sample of the products demonstrates the visual integrity of the line. The simplicity and flexibility of the graphic format allows for the integration of additional flavor offerings.

Existing Wish•Bone image was too busy and lacked clear distinction between individual flavors. As the number of different salad dressings increased, it became more and more difficult to develop meaningful photographic backgrounds.

To reflect a "lite" image for the Wish•Bone line of reduced calorie dressings, a major redesign of the existing line was initiated. The new image, with a clean white background, projects lightness, freshness and appetite appeal via the flavorful vegetable vignette. The color-coded circular image with bold flavor names effectively differentiates products on shelf.

The original packaging failed to position the product line as "lite."

WISH • BONE

Lite

ITALIAN

REDUCED CALORIE DRESSING

8 FL. OZ.
(237 ml)

33

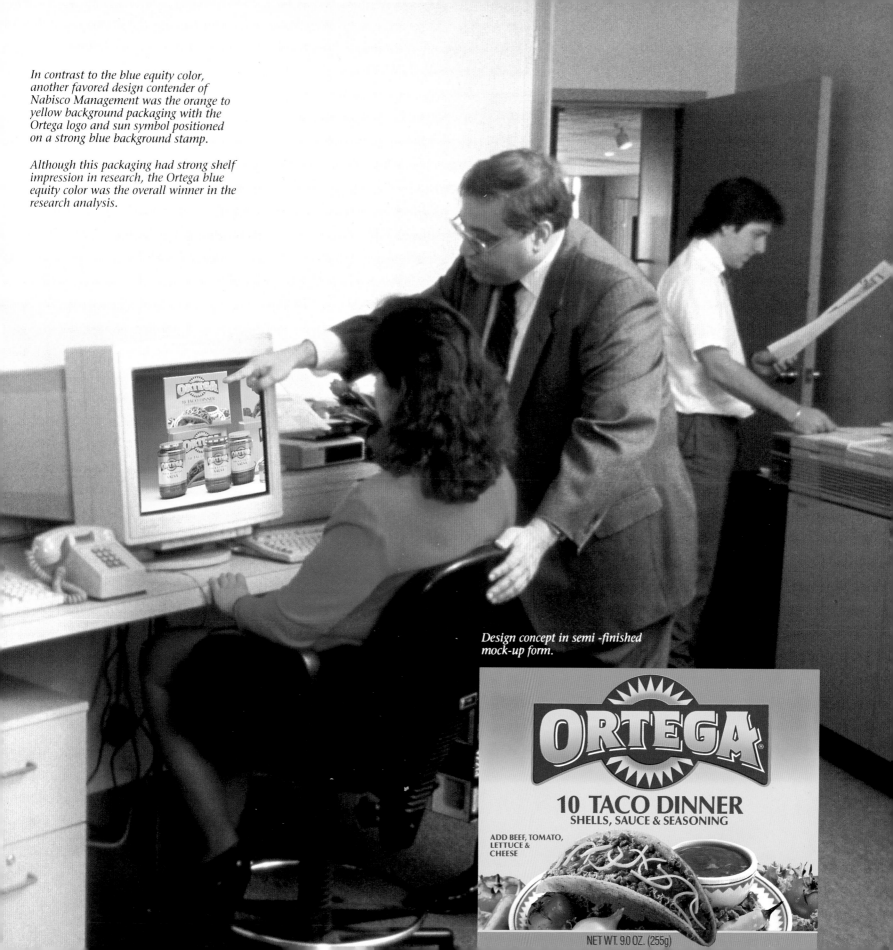

In contrast to the blue equity color, another favored design contender of Nabisco Management was the orange to yellow background packaging with the Ortega logo and sun symbol positioned on a strong blue background stamp.

Although this packaging had strong shelf impression in research, the Ortega blue equity color was the overall winner in the research analysis.

Design concept in semi-finished mock-up form.

ORTEGA

10 TACO DINNER
SHELLS, SAUCE & SEASONING

ADD BEEF, TOMATO, LETTUCE & CHEESE

NET WT. 9.0 OZ. (255g)

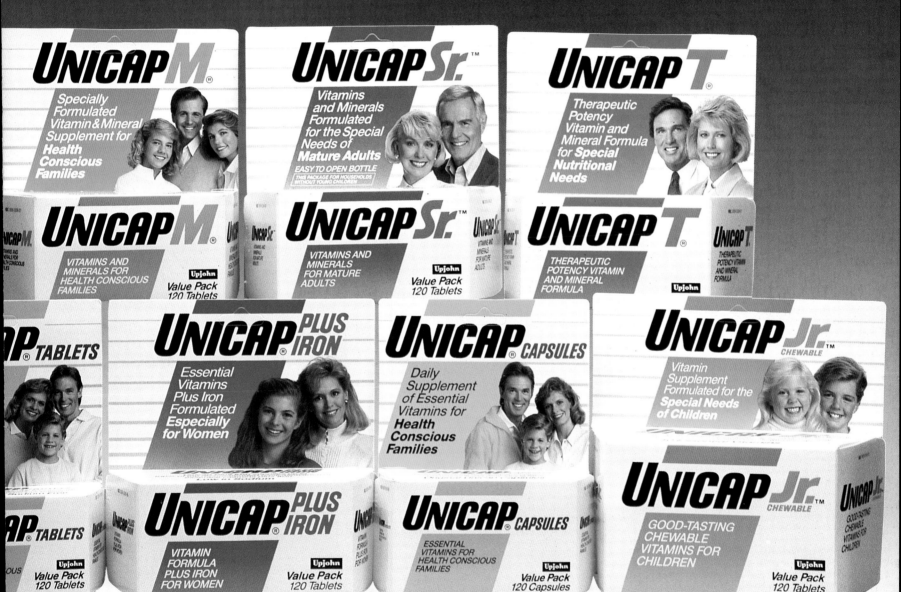

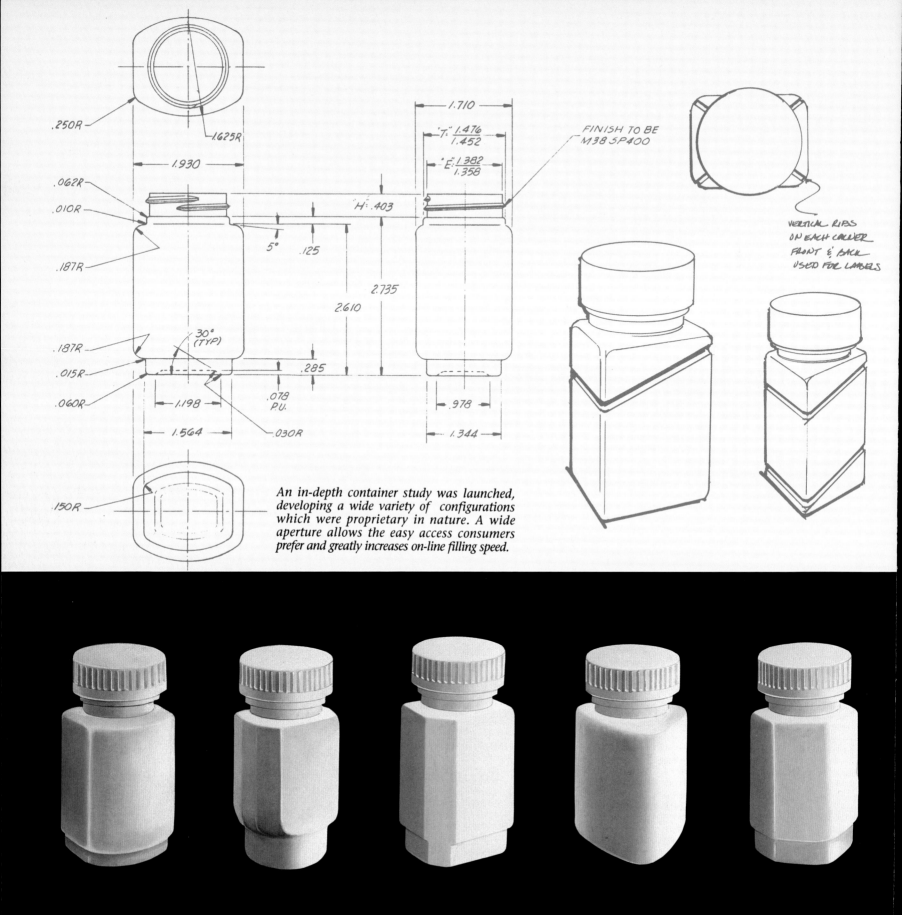

.250R

1.625R

1.930

.062R

.010R

.187R

5° .125

H: .403

2.735

2.610

.187R

30° (TYP)

.015R

.285

.060R

1.198

.078 P.U.

1.564

.030R

.150R

1.710

"T." 1.476
1.452

"E": 1.382
1.358

FINISH TO BE
M38 SP400

VERTICAL RIBS
ON EACH CORNER
FRONT & BACK
USED FOR LABELS

.978

1.344

An in-depth container study was launched, developing a wide variety of configurations which were proprietary in nature. A wide aperture allows the easy access consumers prefer and greatly increases on-line filling speed.

A side-by-side comparison of the old and new imagery conveys the refreshing high quality look that matches the superiority of the product line. The uniquely angled carton, excitingly contemporary in design, presents an eye-catching impression of continuity throughout the line, increasing the highly perceived value of the product. The result is a new, high quality image for Unicap Multi Vitamins and a contemporary look that matches the superiority of the product line. Refreshing, high-tech imagery and carton shape is complemented by the graphic continuity and brand name equity. This image creates a vivid point of purchase impact for the consumer that clearly dominates on-shelf competition. The modern graphics and photography, the concise information and the variety of choices all combine to make Unicap Multi Vitamins a visual standout that guarantees product excellence.

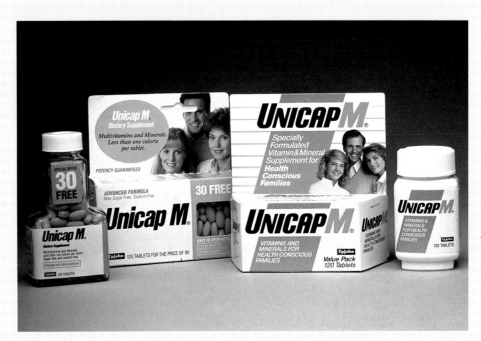

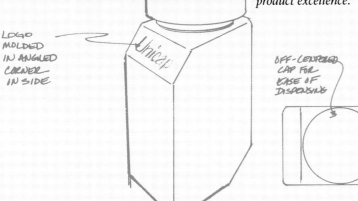

LOGO MOLDED IN ANGLED CORNER INSIDE

OFF-CENTERED CAP FOR EASE OF DISPENSING

The primary container for all Unicap Multi Vitamins, with the exception of Unicap Jr., is made of HDPE plastic for improved efficiency. The curved front and back surfaces, plus the pedestal base, add a contemporary flare of style.

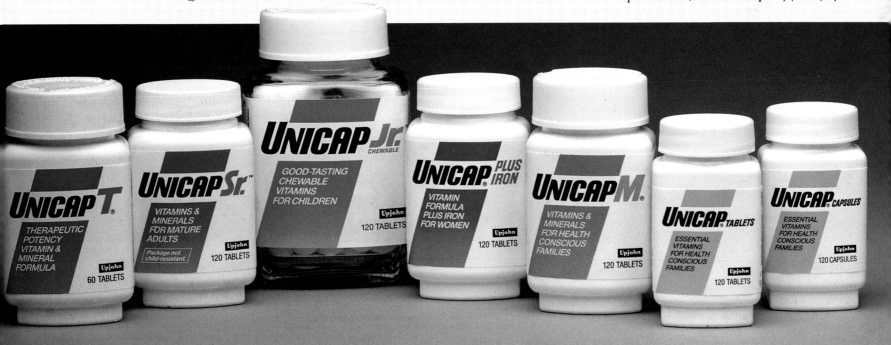

41

The criteria for the redesign of the regular line of salad dressings called for the creation of a more exciting, distinct and contemporary look to reinforce the quality image of Wish•Bone and reflect a strong family relationship with the line of lite products. The rich "Wish•Bone green" background with a strong, circular shape unifies the line, while the full-bodied salad illustration projects appetite appeal.

WISH - BONE™

FAMILY SIZE
ITALIAN
DRESSING

Wi
Bo

Ne
Rec

WISH

RAN
DRES

8 FL. OZ.

To reflect a "lite" image for the Wish•Bone line of reduced calorie dressings, a major redesign of the existing line was initiated. The new image, with a clean white background, projects lightness, freshness and appetite appeal via the flavorful vegetable vignette. The color-coded circular image with bold flavor names effectively differentiates products on shelf.

The original packaging failed to position the product line as "lite."

WISH • BONE

Lite

ITALIAN

REDUCED CALORIE
DRESSING

8 FL. OZ.
(237 ml)

Bottle, used for all Wish•Bone salad dressings, maintains the equity with the original "Wish•Bone" shape.

49

WISH•BONE OLIVE OIL CLASSICS
Thomas J. Lipton Company

CLS&M developed a new line of premium-priced Olive Oil salad dressings which combine an upscale, quality "imported" image while retaining the heritage of the Wish•Bone brand. Continuation of the circular shape motif surrounding the flavor band links the line with the regular and lite Wish•Bone dressings. The illustration of olives imparts a classic, imported feeling.

Creative concepts explored imagery capturing the "look," "feel," and "goodness" associated with imported olive oil.

OLIVE OIL

ITALIAN
OIL BLEND DRESSING

CLASSICS

Wish-Bone.

Imported Olive Oil

OLIVE OIL
ITALIAN
OIL BLEND DRESSING
CLASSICS

8 FL.OZ. (237 ml)

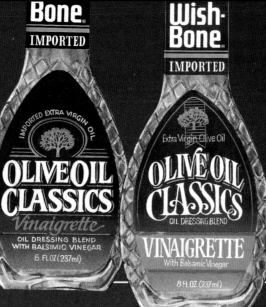

To differentiate the regular olive oil products from the lite products, a rich, gold tone was used in concert with the "Wish•Bone" green, reserving gold on white for the lite line. The overall effect implies good taste and variety of flavor opportunities.

Healthy Sensation! ™

Early rough concepts explored a wide range of innovative graphic formats and logotypes for this new product category.

Today's health-conscious consumers demand sound nutrition and good taste. Healthy Sensations! provides a successful solution. This new line of fat free, cholesterol free, low sodium, reduced calorie dressings are offered in a variety of appetizing flavors. The equity of the rich Wish•Bone green background, a natural choice for a "healthy" product, was enhanced by a spirited italic logotype created by CLS&M. The heritage of the Wish•Bone-shaped bottle and the

Konica's existing line of low-priced cameras were not selling well in the U.S. market. Packaged in a standard blister pack with uninspired graphics, the line was not capturing its target audience—the younger person buying a 35mm camera for the first time. CLS&M was selected to develop an image that would appeal to this young, trendy market. Criteria dictated that the individual cameras had to sell themselves within a mass merchandise outlet. Each of the cameras in the line had to project a unique personality while maintaining a line look. CLS&M positioned the Konica logotype and symbol on the Konica blue background which gradates to white and employs upbeat, contemporary graphic patterns.

Konica®

Konica® 35mm Camera TOMATO

Konica® 35mm Camera EFP 3

- Close-Up Flash Setting
- Easy Loading System
- Focus Free
- Built-In Flash
- Protective Clam Shell Design

- Extra Bright Viewfinder
- Focus Free
- Built-In Flash

The existing packaging, designed and produced in Japan for the U.S. consumer, was unimaginative and did not reflect the desired visual attitude.

All design concepts were executed on computer. A Remote Viewing System was installed at Konica headquarters in New Jersey enabling CLS&M to review favored design candidates with the client and make required modifications.

Competitive products were purchased during store audits and scanned into CLS&M's computers. Each design system we created was positioned in a competitive planogram to enable the client to review each design in a "real world" environment.

Initial design concepts positioned the camera at the same angle as the competition. In the final stages of development, the angle was revised to provide a greater point of difference on shelf.

In a separate study, CLS&M designed the exterior front and back of the camera. Initial concepts were prepared as orthographic projections (front, side and top views) accompanied by three-dimensional renderings.

The individual cameras were hung on racks amid competitive products in the majority of retail outlets. Other stores accepted a 24" merchandiser which accommodated 24 assorted SKU's. The merchandiser functions in a stand-alone position in these self-service environments.

NESTEA ICED TEA
Nestlé USA, Inc.

The Nestlé Foods Company had marketed its Nestea Regular Iced Tea flavor in a package with a green background color for many years. However, as decaffeinated products gained in popularity in many different categories in the supermarket, green became identified as <u>the</u> decaffeinated color. Nestlé decided to reposition its regular flavor, create a new decaffeinated product and prepare for the possibility of a future lemon-flavored product.

The exisiting package was inadvertently communicating decaffeinated.

The new decaffeinated product is differentiated by the strong green background color.

The new package image is inviting, appetizing and promotes the "Take the Nestea Plunge" advertising campaign.

61

Managing Partner Ed Morrill meeting with Senior Designer John Rutig and computer operators Joan Nicosia and Greg Hodgman.

Incorporating the Nestea logotype and "plunge" photography, CLS&M created initial concepts in rough pencil form, scanning them into various computer systems for continued development in color.

Computer technology enabled CLS&M to develop an extensive series of full-color computer line images for the initial Phase I presentation within relatively tight budget and time parameters.

THE TRANSFORMERS
Hasbro Industries, Inc.

One of the toy industry's most successful new product introductions of all time is the Transformers line of robot-action figures. They are, indeed, "More than Meets the Eye!" As a totally unique product concept in the U.S., the packaging graphics had to communicate the dual nature of each product—a car transforming into a futuristic robot and back again—with exciting action-filled images appealing to children ages 5 and "up." Extensive use of air-brushed illustrations combined with close-up photography of the step-by-step transformation process communicate the play value of three toys in one; durability of die-cast vehicles, the fantasy of extra-terrestrial robots and the intrigue of puzzles. Working on an incredibly tight time schedule, even by toy industry standards, CLS&M created logotypes, symbols and high-tech graphics which effectively preempted the category, enabling Hasbro Industries to gain a commanding sales advantage in an extremely competitive environment. Transformers rapidly became the hot item, highly collectible by children of all ages for their novelty, ingenuity and craftsmanship.

Sleek, high-quality airbrushed illustrations portray each Heroic Autobot in a hero's stance. Distortion to perspective and "worm's eye view" angles give the characters an individual personality and larger-than-life attitude.

THE **TRANS FOR**

MORE THAN MEETS THE EYE!

THE TR

MORE THAN MEETS THE EYE! FOR

TRANSFORMS FROM RACE CA TO ROBOT AND BACK!

CITANE

AUTOBOT SPY MIRAGE

64

MERS ®

THE TRANSFORMERS ™

EVIL DECEPTICON

MORE THAN MEETS THE EYE!

TRANSFORMS FROM WALTHER P-38 WEAPON TO ROBOT AND BACK!

TRANS FORMERS ™

HEROIC AUTOBOT

TRACTOR TRAILER TO ROBOT WITH HEADQUARTERS & BACK!

THE TRANSFORMERS ™

EVIL DECEPTICON

MORE THAN MEETS THE EYE!

THE TRANSFORMERS ™

HEROIC AUTOBOT

MORE THAN MEETS THE EYE!

AGES: 5 & UP

ERS ™

THE TRANSFORMERS ™

HEROIC AUTOBOT

MORE THAN MEETS THE EYE!

TRANSFORMS FROM MINICAR TO ROBOT AND BACK!

AUTOBOT BRAWN

TRANSFORMS FROM RACE CAR TO ROBOT AND BACK!

AUTOBOT WARRIOR SUNSTREAKER

AGES: 5 & UP INCLUDES SNAP-ON WEAPONS & ACCESSORIES

65

The existing Tastykake packaging was too busy and was beginning to look dated. Interestingly, this did not effect sales in the Tastykake markets. In fact, the line was enjoying its most profitable year. With the company's loyal consumer base,

the product line could be sold in brown paper bags in its hometown of Philadelphia. The rationale for change came about because the line was not selling as well as competitive national brands in areas of the U.S. where Tastykake was not a known entity.

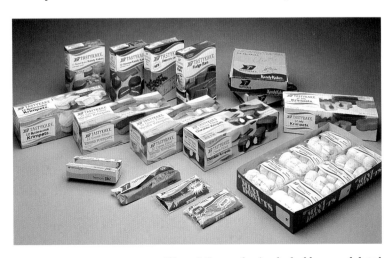

The existing packaging looked busy and dated.

Final design candidate themes were created on computer and adapted to selected product configurations. Analysis of the computer generated shelf-sets provided convincing evidence that the line of products with the yellow background broke through the clutter of competitive imagery most effectively. These concepts were then positioned in plan-ograms alongside competition. Using their computer systems, CLS&M was able to visualize entire line images.

CLS&M developed back panel copy and appetite-appealing illustration to demonstrate the freshly-baked, nutritious ingredients.

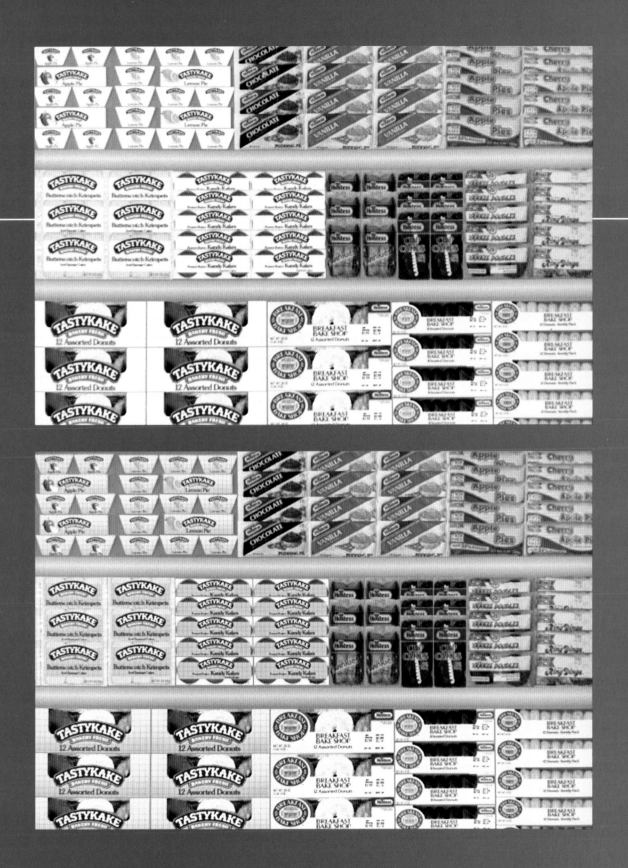

69

The design team determined that the Tastykake logo would be able to stand on its own regardless of background and suggested that "Bakery Fresh" become part of the logo identity. Shield shapes were developed and variations of the original logostyling were implemented in bold formats.

Utilizing photos taken in several store audits on the East Coast, CLS&M was able to present Tastykake Management with the full product line arrangement by piecing together the vaporware images in our Lightspeed computer. The Chairman specifically requested seeing the total merchandiser of new packaging prior to investing in costly separations and engravings.

The computer played a major role in the design and execution of comprehensives. A Remote Viewing System was installed in the client's office in Philadelphia where three-way visual communication was established between the client, CLS&M/NY and the separator, G.S. Imaging, in New Jersey. A quantitative, research study executed by Perception Research Services (PRS) utilized CLS&M's digitized slides of packaging and planograms to measure visual impact of our packaging design theme versus competition. The results led to the new, simplified brand packaging theme which utilizes a grid background with a yellow gradation tone and simple, appetite-appealing photography and illustration.

A 1915 delivery truck reflects the original logostyling. Contemporary rolling stock now has the bold, new Tastykake logo.

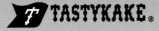

1915 DELIVERY TRUCK

Reynolds®

Reynolds Metals Company had conducted a corporate equity study which confirmed the overpowering strength of its lead brand, Reynolds Wrap. The company has positions in a number of other markets including plastic wrap and plastic bags. In none of these other categories did the Reynolds entry hold the dominant position. CLS&M was asked to develop a new image that would help extend the brand's corporate strength as embodied in Reynolds Wrap.

After an extensive creative development program, a new Reynolds' logo was developed and a system was established that leveraged the Reynolds Wrap look into the other product categories.

Looking at the existing packages, we determined that the uniqueness of the brand images of the Reynolds' products in each category made the brands appear to be individual brand entries.

A consistent presentation of the Reynolds' name and the adoption of a blue background color for all Reynolds' products extended the recognizable strength of the lead brand Reynolds Wrap to not only clearly identify the Reynolds' parentage but also to substantially increase the overall lines' retail shelf impact.

Convenience, ease of preparation and good taste define the direction for the graphic image for a new line of Julienne Potatoes from Betty Crocker.

The Potatoes Express logotype instantly communicates the unique product position. Close-in photography details the delicate Julienne cut of the Idaho Russet potatoes simmered in smooth, delicious sauces.

Strong color-coding for the package backgrounds differentiates the individual flavors.

Positioning each design concept in shelf-sets of the product category allows Marketing Management to visualize the proposed brand images against the competition. The final concept clearly differentiates the new product from the more traditional products in the side dish category.

In a marketplace saturated with new competitors, Contadina's line of fresh pastas, sauces and pizzas was doing extremely well. The Nestlé USA Marketing Group decided, however, that the existing packaging — a dark green circle with the Contadina logo enclosed in a red rectangle — could be more appealing and impactful. They considered upgrading to a more contemporary attitude with an Italian feeling. In some stores the Contadina refrigerated products are grouped in their own section, making for a very powerful display, but since there are stores shelving the pastas, sauces and pizzas separately, the package design had to work independently in strong competitive environments.

Before and after photographs of the Contadina Refrigerated pasta packaging. The green circle was maintained as a major continuation of the existing equity.

A representative photographic sampling of the complete Contadina line for refrigerated pastas, sauces and pizzas with regular and light products.

Contadina recently introduced a new line of Light refrigerated pastas and sauces. CLS&M's planogram methodology assisted marketing management in their focus group research evaluation of the light/cholesterol free category.

and better than the competition. One design, the diamond checkerboard pattern, proved to be significantly better. All mechanical artwork for pastas, sauces and pizzas was produced electronically, utilizing CLS&M's leading-edge Cornerstone computer software technology. Canon color print output from the Macintosh Quadras were sent daily from New York to Los Angeles for final approvals, and CLS&M's remote viewing system was used during the revision stages.

Use By:

Contadina
Cheese Pizza Kit

Create Freshly Baked Pizza in Minutes

Pizza Crust • Pizza Sauce

Mozzarella Cheese
Shredded Part-Skim

REAL · 100% REAL CHEESE

New!

Make Your Favorite Pizza to Order in Minutes

Freshly Baked with the Finest Ingredients & No Preservatives

Contadina
Pizza Crust

Keep Refrigerated
May Be Frozen

Use By:

Preparation Instructions: Add your favorite sauce, cheese and toppings for a piping hot pizza that is made to order; or brush with olive oil and sprinkle with herbs and cheese for a delicious, new spin on garlic bread. Bake directly on middle rack in a preheated 425° oven for 8-10 minutes. . . and Serve!

Ingredients: Bleached enriched flour (flour, malted barley flour, niacin, reduced iron, thiamine mononitrate, riboflavin) water, salt, sugar, yeast, partially hydrogenated soybean oil and olive oil.

Nestlé Refrigerated Food Company,
Glendale, CA 91203

Questions or Comments? Please save package and call 1-800-727-0050 (Mon.-Fri., 8am-4pm Pacific Time)

0 00000 00000 0

NET WT. 10.5 OZ.

The new Contadina graphic image is equally impactful on the pizza line. Appetite-appealing photography of pizza with cheese and toppings enhances the visual appeal of the package.

The line was expanded to include an individual pizza crust product positioned in a plastic wrap. This product is accompanied in some store displays with individual Contadina toppings of cheese, sausage, pepperoni, etc.

The 3M Company, the company that has brought us SCOTCH TAPE and POST-IT notepads, has long been known for its expertise in research and development. Recently they applied their technological acumen to a totally new category with the development of a system of 24 products for the do-it-yourself wood refinishing market.

Safest Stripper™

Safest Stripper™
Paint and Varnish Remover (Semi-Paste)
• No harmful fumes • Use indoors or out
• No gloves required
CAUTION! Causes irritation of eyes on contact.
Carefully read caution on back
1 Pint (16 OZ.) .473 Liters
3M
Cat. 10100

Safest Stripper™
and Varnish
(Semi-Paste)

Final Stripping Pads
For Residue Removal
• Effectively removes paint residue without harming wood
• Replaces "O" steel wool
• Won't shred, splinter or rust
Contents: 2 pads
6" x 3⅞"
(152mm x 98mm)
3M
Cat. 10113

1 handle
1 pad
3½" x 5" x ½"
(88mm x 127mm)

Heavy Duty Stripping Pads
• Use with chemical paint strippers
• Removes paints, varnishes and other finishes without harming wood
• Won't splinter or shred like steel wool
Contents: 2 pads
6" x 3⅞"
(152mm x 98mm)
3M
Cat. 10112

Heavy Duty Stripping Pads
• Use with chemical paint strippers
• Removes paints, varnishes and other finishes without harming wood
• Replacement pads for 3M Stripping Tool
Contents: 2 pads
3½" x 5" x ½"
(88mm x 127mm x 12.7mm)
3M
Cat. 10111

Just Like Wood™
Wood Putty
• Dries quickly
• Apply directly from tu
• Durable and long-las

Very Fine
Flex
Sand
Pad
Provides super
on curved, roun
detailed surface
Contents: 1 Pad
2⅞" x 3⅞" x ⅝"
(73mm x 98.4mm x 15.8r
3M
Cat. 10128

3M

CLS&M was brought in to consult on the line in its early stages and as a first step worked closely with the client to source stock containers and help develop structures for the entire line. This was particularly difficult due to the diversity of packaging forms. In addition to stock High-Density Polyethylene (HDPE) and a high-tech custom bottle with a special barrier and special child resistant closures, the project called for the development of folding cartons, paperboard sleeves and simple, fan fold instructional labels.

The products in this 24 item line were grouped into three separate categories as part of a product use system. CLS&M developed label graphics that used coded color "Swipes" for each of these categories to help tie together the product groupings. The first group of products is used to strip the old finish from the furniture.

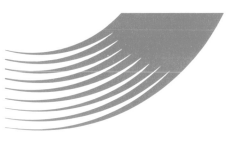

The second group of products is used to prepare the surface for the new finish.

The third group of products is used to apply the final finish and help clean up.

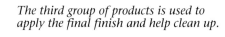

84

Graphic design concepts (above and below) were developed on the computer. Type, photography and graphic images were easily repositioned and reproportioned by special programming.

To clearly describe each product, type selection and special label configurations were developed on the computer.

Offering a complete family of products was important to 3M's marketing strategy. To tie this family of products together from a graphics standpoint, a design system was developed. A high quality, contemporary image was needed to help distinguish the look of the 3M line from the traditional look of the competitors. In the selected design, the 3M logo is used as an endorsement of quality. A black structural color reinforces the strong label impact.

Expanding the computer usage into the merchandising area, CLS&M developed special end cap displays simulating in-store configurations. Initial rough computer visualizations of these multi-product displays enabled the client to refine the packaging before it reached the final production stage (see computer illustration below).

Final computer merchandising concepts were executed in a simulated in-store environment by cloning the individual package designs to form multiple facings on-shelf (see computer photograph below).

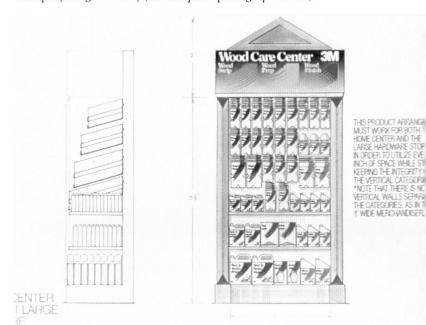

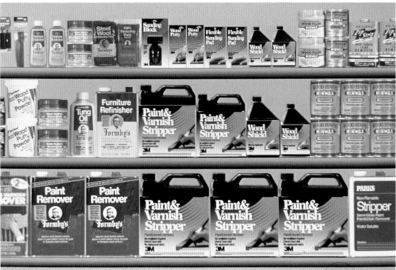

Lightspeed computer-generated 35mm digital slides were prepared of store planograms to show how each of the proposed new 3M Wood Refinishing line design concepts would compete on-shelf within the competitive clutter.

The Optel Remote Viewing System played a major role in the communication of this design program. From start to finish, the three-dimensional structural development and packaging graphics for this important 3M Company design program had to be completed in eleven months so that the new product line could be introduced at the National Hardware Show.

3M Director of Corporate Communications, Linda Keefe, at her office in Minneapolis, reviews an in-store display design with Owen W. Coleman and John Chrzanowski. During the final production stages, three-way remote viewing was taking place daily between CLS&M's computer system designers in New York, 3M design management in Minneapolis and the production staff at Techtron Packaging, the electronic color separator, based in Chicago.

The overall high-tech imagery of the packaging was extended to the corrugated shipping units. To allow retailers to build free-standing and on-shelf displays, special cut-case corrugates carrying the high-tech look of the individual product packages were developed.

Just Like Wood™
Wood Putty

3M
Cat. 10134

Wood Refinisher's
Tack Cloth

3M
24 Pieces
QTY./B.U.
3M I.B. NO
70-07-10132-2
51111-10132-2
Cat. 10132

Wood Refinisher's
Tack Cloth

Removes dust, dirt, lint and other particles to help achieve super smooth surfaces

3M
Cat. 10132

Just Like Wood™
Wood Putty

• Dries quickly
• Apply directly fr
• Durable and lor

• Dries quickly
• Apply directly from tube
• Durable and long-lasting

CAUTION! May cause eye
irritation. (see back panel)
Content: 1 tube

NET WT. 3.5 OZ. (99.2g)

3M
Cat. 10134

Applies directly from tube
Dries quickly

3M

Wood Refinisher's
Tack Cloth

• Removes dust, dirt, lint and other particles to help achieve super smooth surfaces

Contents: 17 in. x 36 in.
(43.2cm x 91.4 cm)
Single Ply 612 sq. in.

3M
Cat. 10132

The marketing direction set for this line called for an image that conveyed "technology of the '90's." CLS&M conducted a visual audit of competitive products and existing shelf set-ups around the country. Since the competition presented a folksier, homier-type image, the graphics development program for the 3M line reached for a more technologically oriented presentation.

Smart eating, regular exercise and stress management are concerns of everyone in the nineties. Today's consumers are making intelligent decisions and long-term commitments to healthy, nutritious and easy-to-follow programs of diet and exercise. Pritikin is a simple, step-by-step plan combining good foods, exercise and stress reduction techniques to insure health and energy for life. CLS&M's challenge was to develop an identity that would encompass this lifestyle approach to good health, while conveying the wholesome freshness and unique character of a line of over 50 products. A strong family identification had to be carried across the line, while enabling each individual category to stand independently on the shelf. The brand personality was created to promote Pritikin's distinctive qualities, unique characteristics and healthy intentions to a target audience receptive to the scope of the program.

The crisp, clean look of the Pritikin brand mark and the fresh appeal of the packaging provide a visual stimulus for the consumer. Its message of fresh, natural ingredients for sound nutrition combined with exercise and stress management is communicated rapidly and simply, and is summarized in its product statement, "Live your life in your prime." The logo is immediately recognizable on product packaging, signage, T-shirts and various applications.

ritikin®

LIFE   IN YOUR PRIME

Package face panel comprehensives were created incorporating favored brand logo-types.

Graphic study explored appetite-appealing photography versus illustration.

Old packaging did not communicate the lifestyle attributes of the line.

A computer planogram was created incorporating an existing Pritikin package.

Each final concept was viewed against competition.

The uniqueness of this brand mark concept becomes evident.

The package design had to adapt to the various configurations of this 50 product line including bottle labels for salad dressings, labels for canned soups, boxes for cereals, pastas and rice products, polybags and foil packets for dips

Simple, yet elegant typographic styling combines with the clean, fresh Pritikin logo-type and symbol of the energetic "Pritikin person" on a variety of hot cereal products. The appetizing photography suggests early morning sunrise and the promise to start the day in a wholesome way.

Adapting the image to different container shapes in computer concept form.

Cloning initial concepts on computer allows for evaluation of multiple imagery

Final electronic mechanical artwork created on the Mac incorporating digitized die geometry received by modem from Laserpoint.

The very first all-panel layout was prepared in traditional black and white pencil form.

Ability of computer to clone images to get a preview of the extended line look.

FRENCH'S SPICE LINE
Durkee French Foods

Consumer research conducted by the Durkee French Company indicated that although

the use of spices was increasing, shopping for them was a difficult, confusing process. Shoppers had a hard time differentiating between the various jars, tins and cartons and they desired more usage information on the label. These difficulties hindered impulse sales and made inventory management a headache. Since the spice line was to be marketed in some regions as French's and in others as Durkee's, logo and graphic adaptaions had to be considered to accommodate both. The graphics were contemporized to make them unique and appealing. The logos "French's" or "Durkee" had to instantly stand out and the entire line had to be organized into a system that would make shopping simple and enjoyable.

Existing line prior to upgrade design program.

Durkee

easonings

Color coding proved an effective way to categorize the spices into five sub-groups, reflecting their various uses; orange for baking spices and extracts, red for cooking spices, green for garlic and onion products, gray for peppers and blue for specialty seasonings.

Shop by Color
- Cooking Spices
- Baking Spices & Extracts
- Specialty Seasonings
- Pepper (All Types)
- Garlic & Onion Products

Creative concepts explore various design solutions in semi-finished comprehensive mock-up form.

A unique, hand-lettered alphabet was created and content identifiers were executed to match the already familiar logos.

Three sets of double line borders were added—two framing the spice name and one extending from both sides of the logo, making it more contemporary and noticeable.

An illustration of each spice was added to provide further clarity, drama and flavor appeal.

CLS&M created a new Ultra Trend detergent package which was positioned in supermarkets where the regular Trend packaging did not appear. Several visual package design audits were initially conducted to review competitive ultra products like Gain, Dash, Rinso and Arm & Hammer. Critical to the new graphics was the development of a pre-price visual statement, since an important strategic rationale for marketing the Ultra Trend product was the price point. The packaging was created with strong, bold diagonal banners utilizing day-glo colors for a powerful shelf impression at point of purchase.

The Ultra Trend image had to relate graphically to the regular Trend detergent.

(Below) Several face panel design concepts were prepared in full color comprehensive form and were presented to Dial Management in multiple format planograms next to competition.

Bold, impactful graphics were carried across several packaging sizes. The Ultra Trend logo was developed in a positive format to assist in distinguishing it from the regular detergent line.

Inspired by fine cuisine from around the world, the Green Giant division of Pillsbury created a new line of frozen vegetable mixtures which combine exceptional tasting sauce flavors with distinctive world-class vegetable combinations. Sauces are packaged in a revolutionary, two-compartment configuration providing a remarkable, pre-blended quality to the sauces. The classic lettering style of the International Mixtures logotype and the international symbols reflect the upscale positioning of the product.

Store audits of the frozen food category revealed the need for a unique logotype that could break through clutter while communicating ease of preparation. This was achieved with the bold italic classic lettering style of the logo and the illustration of the sauce packet on the polybag. The heritage of the Green Giant brand and the Green Giant "sea of green" form the backdrop for the carefully-styled product photography.

For quick flavor differentiation, color-coded panels are tied together with close-up photography of the product on a spoon.

The criteria and objectives of the design project allowed for a variety of creative concepts shown above in semi-rough layouts.

In the highly competitive environment of self-service discount stores, the packaging has to be the salesman. To this end, Corning dinnerware products have been restaged by CLS&M, enhancing the strong brand equity of the Corelle name and leveraging the heritage and quality associated with Corning. An umbrella image was created to unify the line of over 30 products. Differentiation of the price-point segments was improved by developing category names and color-coded graphics.

CORELL

IMAGES
DINNERWARE BY **CORNI**

Ed Morrill, Managing Partner of CLS&M, makes one of several design concept presentations to Corning Management. The presentations included the visualization of each final line image candidate in multiples in competitive shelf sets, greatly facilitating the selection of the most effective line images.

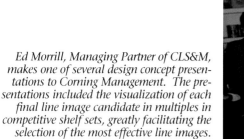

Store audits confirmed the need for a cleaner, more organized and simplified presentation of the wide range of patterns, piece counts, colors and shapes offered.

CORELLE® IMPRESSIONS™
DINNERWARE BY CORNING

PASTEL BALLET™
ELEGANTLY EMBOSSED
20 PIECE SET · SERVICE FOR 4
FOR DINING WITH DISTINCTION

CORELLE® IMAGES™
DINNERWARE BY CORNING

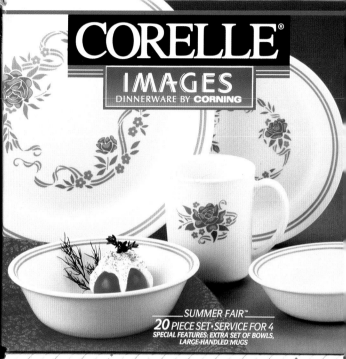

SUMMER FAIR™
20 PIECE SET · SERVICE FOR 4
SPECIAL FEATURES: EXTRA SET OF BOWLS,
LARGE-HANDLED MUGS

CORELLE® Casuals™
DINNERWARE BY CORNING

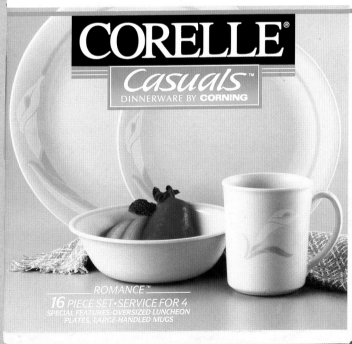

ROMANCE™
16 PIECE SET · SERVICE FOR 4
SPECIAL FEATURES: OVERSIZED LUNCHEON
PLATES, LARGE-HANDLED MUGS

CORELLE® LIVINGWARE™
BY CORNING

*Timeless Looks,
Proven Durability*

APRICOT GROVE™

16 PIECE SET · SERVICE FOR 4
CONTAINS FOUR EACH:
10 1/4" DINNER PLATES
6 3/4" BREAD AND BUTTER PLATES
18 OZ. SOUP/CEREAL BOWLS
8 OZ. TAPERED MUGS

Since 1921 the Filtered Water Service Corporation has been serving the New York metropolitan area and has built a substantial business under that trusted name. As consumers' appetites for pure drinking water rapidly increased, the management of Filtered Water Service Corporation focused their efforts to reach these individuals in addition to the many corporations they were servicing. This could be achieved, they felt by revitalizing their image. The SnowBird name and new brand identity created by CLS&M included the "Pure Clean Water" descriptor which clearly conveys the image desired by the company's management.

Pure clear wa

Delivery trucks are major image builders for water companies. The clean, refreshing SnowBird image is seen everyday on the streets of the New York area.

The graphics have been adapted for use on a wide variety of materials including stationery, business forms, paper drinking cups, promotional items and uniforms.

SnowBird
Pure clear water ™

FILTERED WATER SERVICE CORP.
419 West 55th Street
New York, N.Y. 10019

May 13, 1992

Mr. Ed Morrill
Coleman, Lipuma, Segal, & Morrill, Inc.
305 East 46th Street
New York, New York

Dear Ed:

It is with great pride that we write this letter to you on our new SnowBird stationery.

We would like to express our sincere thanks today to you for creating the beautiful image of SnowBird and helping us adopt it for our stationery, bottles and trucks.

All of our employees and the customers who have seen it have told us that the design portrays the pure clean image we want for our Bottled water.

Working with you and your design staff has been a real pleasure.

We look forward to other projects as we adapt your design for different items.

Sincerely,

FILTERED WATER SERVICE CORP.

Diane Drey, President

FILTERED WATER SERVICE CORP.

Computer technology was fully utilized in the development of graphics for the many different styles of rolling stock. Throughout the program computers played an important role in design concept adaptations and in the preparation of final mechanical artwork in electronic digital format, including films and negatives for printing.

Initial rough concepts explored a wide range of fresh new visual directions from which to choose both symbol and logotype combinations.

TAMPAX®

CLS&M created a brand image for a new European tampon product called Tampets which is endorsed by the Tampax name. The use of planograms for each major European market enabled marketing executives to select a single, global design within forty-five minutes. At a meeting in New York with Tambrands senior management from each country, CLS&M Europe's Managing Partner in the U.K., Steve Merry, presented several package design concepts. As each was moved from country to country on the individual planograms, Tambrands' executives were reassured that the new package design could work in each country and came to an agreement in record time.

Ward Hooper, CLS&M Design Director, advises members of the Tampets design team during the development of the new brand image.

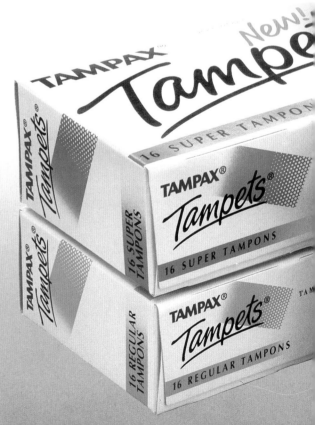

The package design incorporates a bold diagonal band with a graphic pattern to indicate absorbency. European color codes distinguish the regular from the super absorbency product.

113

Duplicate computer planogram boards are prepared for the client and designer. Work in progress can be reviewed both in New York and at the client's office in the United Kingdom.

CLS&M's New York design team and principals review the various aspects of the Tambrands design program. (R to L), Anne Swan, Owen Coleman, Karen Corell, Lorraine Fierro, Abe Segal, Eileen Ferara, William Lee and John Rutig.

A major conceptual design study was presented in the initial design phase. Package designs were presented individually and in multiple formats as they would appear on-shelf in supermarkets.

Large size planogram boards representing each country were executed showing the "real life" clutter of the competitive shelf sets.

CLS&M President, Owen W. Coleman, positions full-color design concepts on each country's representative planogram during the initial presentation.

CLS&M Europe recently completed the re-design of several important product lines for the Findus Division of Nestlé Ltd. in the U.K. The Crispy Pancake packaging was simplified with a strong flavor name identification combined with color coding and appetite-appealing

Findus ®

photography. All design themes were created within new Findus brand name packaging guidelines. Visual communication on this initial design assignment was established by three-way Optel remote viewing. Initial concepts were reviewed with our partner, Steve Merry, in the U.K. with final design directions reviewed at our client's offices in Croydon, U.K.

Principal Abe Segal directs a revision in the electronic artwork to Computer Designer, Larry Aaron.

Findus

Fish Provençale
With a Tomato, Onion & Red Pepper Sauce

2 Individually Wrapped Fillets

New!

2x225g

Serving Suggestion

10 Pack

Grill, Fry & NOW Ovenable

Findus

Crispy Pancakes
with Chicken & Mushroom Filling

10 Pack

Grill, Fry & NOW Ovenable

Crispy Pancakes
with Cheddar Cheese Filling

Serving Suggestion

Final electronic separations and printing were executed in the U.K. using Mac Quadra Cornerstone software.

Findus

Fish Moutarde
With a Wholegrain Mustard Sauce

2 Individually Wrapped Fillets

New!

2x225g

Serving Suggestion

Findus

Fish Parisienne
With a Creamy Mushroom Sauce

2 Individually Wrapped Fillets

New!

2x225g

Serving Suggestion

Crosse & Blackwell Management decided to contemporize their existing brand of 26 seasoning mixes. CLS&M Europe, initially working with one of the flavors, developed a broad design exploratory, tying the new sub-brand name, "Simply Fix," to the Crosse & Blackwell range brand image. Based upon a review of competitive products, it was critical to develop a simple design format — typographically and through strong appetite-appealing visuals which would enable the consumer to easily identify the individual recipe items. Our design teams in the U.S. and the U.K. determined that red was a critical equity color for Crosse & Blackwell packaging. The actual-size competitive planograms were set up based upon store audits conducted in the U.K.

QUALITY at LOW PRICES

CLS&M Europe's Managing Partner, Steve Merry, reviews existing Crosse & Blackwell packaging in several store audits in the U.K.

Planograms were duplicated for our designers' and client's review in both the U.S. and U.K. From the inception of this important study, each design concept was reviewed and presented to management in multiple formats on shelf.

121

The favored package design candidate theme is reviewed by Principals Owen W. Coleman (left) and Abe Segal with Project Director, Cathy SzeTu in New York.

Colman's Casserole — Traditional **Sausage Casserole** — Colman's Casseroles

Colman's Casserole Mix for Chicken — **Chicken Chasseur** — Colman's Casseroles

Colman's Casserole Mix for Chicken — **Coq au Vin** — Mix to Add to Chicken & Vegetables Before Cooking — Colman's Casseroles

Colman's Casserole Mix for Beef — Traditional **Beef Casserole** — Colman's Casseroles

Colman's Casserole Mix for Pork — Traditional **Pork Casserole** — Colman's Casseroles

CROSSE & BLACKWELL *Simply Fix* — **Sweet & Sour Chicken** SEASONING MIX — Add to Chicken, Pineapple and Peppers — MICROWAVEABLE

CROSSE & BLACKWELL *Simply Fix* — **Sweet & Sour Chicken** SEASONING MIX — Add to Chicken, Pineapple and Peppers — MICROWAVEABLE

CROSSE & BLACKWELL *Simply Fix* — **Chicken à la King** SEASONING MIX — Add to Chicken, Vegetables and Milk — MICROWAVEABLE

CROSSE & BLACKWELL *Simply Fix* — **Chicken à la King** SEASONING MIX — Add to Chicken, Vegetables and Milk — MICROWAVEABLE

CROSSE & BLACKWELL *Simply Fix* — STIR... Sweet & Sour **Pork** — Add to Pork, Canned Pineapple, Vegetables for a Complete Stir...

CROSSE & BLACKWELL COOK-IN-THE-POT **CASSEROLE** — A casserole mix for **Vegetable Curry** — Simply add to mixed vegetables, milk and water — CROSSE & BLACKWELL

CROSSE & BLACKWELL **STIR FRY** mix for **Beef Satay** — CROSSE & BLACKWELL

CROSSE & BLACKWELL COOK-IN-THE-POT **CASSEROLE** — A casserole mix for **Barbecue Chicken** — Simply add to chicken and vegetables — CROSSE & BLACKWELL

CROSSE & BLACKWELL COOK-IN-THE-POT **CASSEROLE** — A casserole mix for **Beef Goulash** — Simply add to beef and vegetables — **Beef Goulash**

CROSSE & BLACKWELL **MICROWAVE** Chicken Korma — A recipe dish mix specially created for the microwave — simply add to chicken, cream and water — 15 MINUTES

CROSSE & BLACKWELL *Simply Fix* ...ROLE

CROSSE & BLACKWELL *Simply Fix* — **Chili con Carne** SEASONING MIX — Add to Mixed beef, Onion, Tomatoes and kidney beans — MICROWAVEABLE

SAFEWAY POUR-OVER **Curry sauce mix** — just add water

SAFEWAY Cook-in sauce mix — **Chicken Chass...** — just add to meat... before...

During the design process, minor changes were executed and reviewed through remote viewing systems located at our offices in New York and London. Mr. Merry supervised and directed all appetite-appealing photography in the U.K. while electronic mechanical art-work was executed in the U.S.

CLS&M redesigned the most popular children's/all-family filled cookie in France. Utilizing our computer remote viewing capabilities, competitive products were sent to us from Paris and local markets and scanned into our Lightspeed computers. LU Marketing Management was able to review each initial design concept in position next to other French supermarket products. The new upscale design theme added a stronger quality reference across flavors. The new design has been extremely well received not only by the Parisiennes, but throughout Europe.

Several design concepts and logo brand name styles were reviewed within the computer package design process.

The LU brand image, originally established by Raymond Lowey many years ago, has been changed modestly since it has major long-term equity. It is one of the most powerful brand marks on shelf in multiple formats.

Several concepts were created and positioned within computer planograms for the upgrade of the Figolu brand.

The final packaging design (below) was carried across the original well-established fig flavor and extended to the Fruits des Bois (mixed fruit flavored bar). Appetite appeal was achieved with super-realistic, full-color illustration of the fruits.

Revitalizing a major brand while maintaining equity with the current packaging is a challenging assignment. It requires a special sensitivity to—and focus on—the individual elements as well as the overall packaging image. The evolutionary new brand image communicates higher quality, while retaining consumer confidence in the product. This was achieved with new physical packaging incorporating the new Colgate brand logotype with upgraded flavor symbols and an enhanced color code system.

Early rough concepts explored a wide variety of possible directions.

The existing packaging was the "jumping off point" from which all new concepts were developed. The final design is more contemporary and impactful at point-of-purchase.

A new umbrella image was created for Nestlé USA's dry pasta and tomato product lines. Although each product line is positioned in a different place in the supermarket, it was CLS&M's challenge to tie the lines together through graphics.

The existing United States Buitoni packaging was redesigned to fit more closely to European Buitoni imagery.

New packaging for Dalla Casa Buitoni/Contadina products was carried across 12 dry pasta products and 29 tomato products.

Design Management at Nestlé SA in Vevey, Switzerland played a major role in marrying the European Buitoni image with the Contadina lady. The Dalla Casa Buitoni seal of quality, currently positioned throughout Europe was tied together in a strong trademark seal with Contadina. This quality trademark forms the cornerstone of both the dry pastas and tomato products. Nestlé Vevey guidelines were also implemented for color gradation tones and gold diagonal lines. Appetite-appealing photography added to the overall quality feel of the packaging.

CASTROL GTX
Castrol Inc.

Castrol is a worldwide leader in motor oil technology and Castrol GTX super multi-grade motor oil is perhaps the most recognized brand image in its category. CLS&M developed and fine-tuned packaging graphics to communicate quality, dependability and state-of-the-art product engineering. Bold typography combined with Castrol orange and green color bands suggest a racing circuit heritage. Extending the equity in the color and graphic format to a wide range of product forms and uses unifies the line and provides highly effective synergy at point-of-sale.

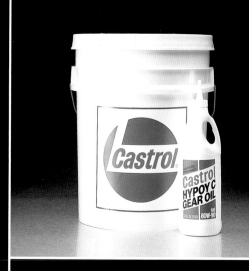

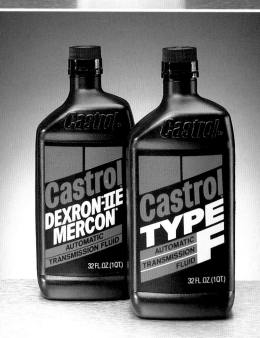

To effectively position Syntec—a new motor oil product from Castrol, Inc.—as a unique, technologically advanced product, CLS&M developed visually impactful imagery emphasizing the product's high-tech, superior performance attributes. The silver metallic graphics and logostyling on a black background reflect the product's high quality and distinguish it amid a very cluttered and confusing environment. CLS&M used silver stamping for a high-gloss, metallic look—unusual for this product category.

The six-pack carton provides a large surface area to effectively billboard the new image.

The logo can be seen on various point-of-purchase displays including shelf-talkers, hats, jackets, banners, posters and t-shirts. CLS&M created a totally new look in the automotive category with a graphics system visually consistent with this technologically advanced, high-tech lubricant.

A dramatic bottle-shaped display unit standing 6 ft in height holds individual products as well as six-pack cartons.

Reminiscent of racing checks, the green imagery represents and reinforces the unique molecular bonding quality of Syntec. The checked pattern imparts a feeling of fluidity of motion and action. Although abstract, the graphics were easily recognizable and could be translated to various promotional materials.

One of the most competitive categories in the H&BA area is cough remedies. The multiplicity of package sizes and product formulations makes packaging communications difficult. Robitussin is the leading cough remedy in the U.S.A. To maintain its leadership position in the face of intense competition CLS&M was asked to study the brand's packaging, evaluate existing equities and develop a new overall look for the line.

A·H·ROBINS

Robitussin ®

CLS&M built upon the recognizable features of the existing package and raised the overall ethical image of the brand. A design format was developed to allow for brand extensions setting up a consistent logo that could carry over to new products and forms.

A review of existing packaging highlighted the fact that the brand logo was presented in a number of different formats and colors. The package also had identical front and back panels which unnecessarily limited space available to provide important consumer product information.

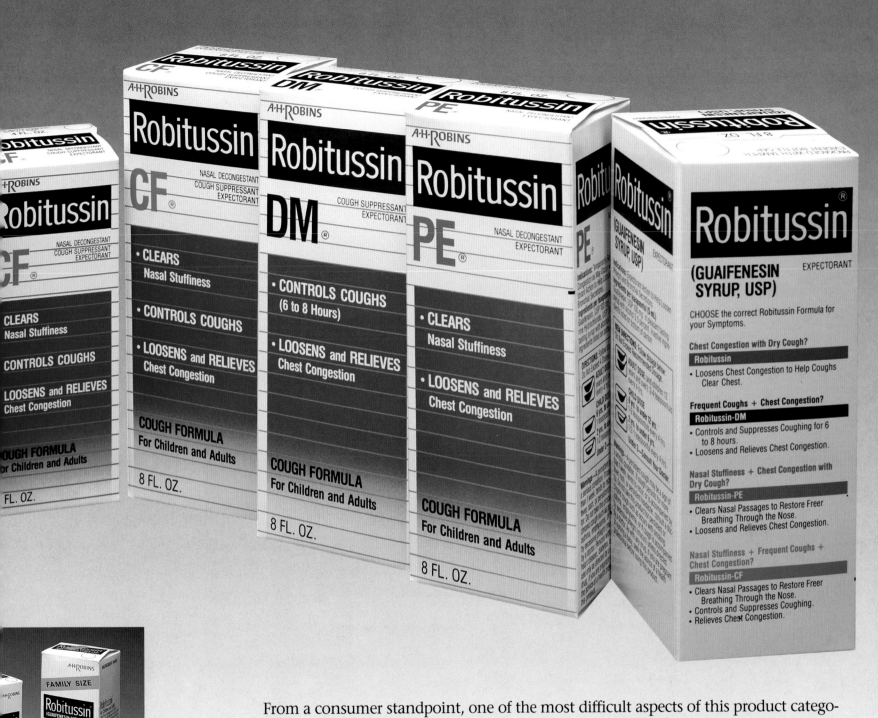

From a consumer standpoint, one of the most difficult aspects of this product category is to match the relief offered by the various formulations to the consumer's symptoms. One of the important elements of the CLS&M redesign effort was to provide a display format clearly defining the way each formulation works. A consistent presentation of the Robitussin logo, and stronger color-coded formulation designators—CF, DM and PE—were developed. Working with a technical writer, CLS&M developed clearer, crisper explanations for each product and devoted an entire panel on each to cross-sell other available formulations, developing add-on sales for the brand.

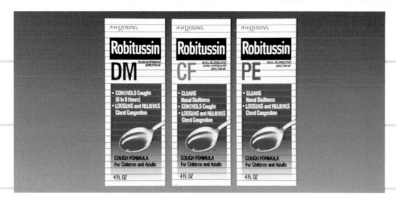

A wide variety of concepts were developed during the exploratory phase.

2/16/88 Robitussin Plan

CLS&M's unique planogram methodology used during the developmental phase was also help[...] in evaluating potential designs for the Robitussin cough drops line extension.

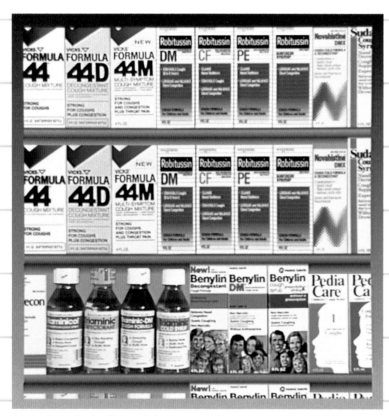

Throughout the developmental program, each concept was positioned within a computer-generated competitive planogram to reflect the "real world" retail setting in which each of the designs would have to compete.

5 Revise 3 Final

After the selection of the final design for the cough remedy, a new exploratory was initiated for the line of Robitussin cough drops.

3c

Designs close to the cough remedy i[...] and other more revolutionary theme[...] part of the initial exploratory.

Incorporating the strong black and white Robitussin logo , the final design utilized a color coding system which clearly identified the Robitussin cough drops parentage, while allowing the product to compete within the cough drop category.

7 Revise 3d Final

ZODIAC
Zoecon Corporation

Zodiac is the leading line of flea and tick products sold through the pet shop trade. Consumer research of existing packaging suggested that there was room for substantial improvement of the packaging in the area of overall imagery and shelf impact. Since the packaging served as the primary consumer contact for this non-advertised brand, CLS&M was asked to do a complete overhaul of the brand's personality with primary objectives being to improve the brand's professional/ethical imagery and make the package design more consumer friendly.

ZODIAC® STEP 1
ZODIAC STEP 2
ZODIAC STEP 3
ZODIAC STEP 4
PET PROTECTION PROGRAM

Perception Research Services' research of the existing packaging suggested the opportunity to totally revise the logo and overall "feel" of the package. An additional objective was recommended by CLS&M to highlight the 4-Step Guarantee Program which had been introduced as the keystone of the brand's overall marketing effort.

ZODIAC®
PET PROTECTION

ZODIAC® For Dogs with necks to 25"
5 Month Flea & Tick Collar With One-Piece Buckle

ZODIAC® STEP 2

PET PROTECTION PROGRAM

5 Month
Flea & Tick Collar
With One-Piece Buckle
FOR DOGS

Kills fleas & ticks
up to 5 months

ACTIVE INGREDIENT:
o-Isopropoxyphenyl
methylcarbamate 9.4%
INERT INGREDIENTS: 90.6%

Do not allow children
to play with this collar
CAUTION
See cautions on back

NET WT. 1.2 OZ. (34g)

ZODIAC® For Cats of all sizes
Flea Collar

ZODIAC® STEP 2

PET PROTECTION PROGRAM

Flea Collar
FOR CATS

Kills fleas

ACTIVE INGREDIENT:
Carbaryl (1-Naphthyl
N-methylcarbamate) 8.5%
INERT INGREDIENTS: 91.5%

Keep out of reach of children
CAUTION
See cautions on back

NET WT. 0.4 OZ. (11.3g)

Appealing full-color illustrations were created for all of the on-animal type products and positioned against bold color-coded brush strokes to further differentiate dog and cat products.

The new Zodiac line imagery substantially increased the brand's shelf impact and strongly conveyed a much more professional/ethical look. The new packages also clearly differentiate those products designed to be used on-animal from those products designed for use in the animal's environment.

ZODIAC ~~STEP~~ **3**
PET PROTECTION PROGRAM

Yard & Kennel Spray

ONCENTRATE

s Ticks & Fleas

WITH SPECIAL
APPLICATOR

tains Dursban®

out of reach of children.
~~C~~TION
ck panel for additional precautionary statements.

OZ. (1PT.) 473 ml

ZODIAC ~~STEP~~ **1**
PET PROTECTION PROGRAM

Pro Dip II
Sponge-on or Dip
FOR DOGS

Controls fleas
& ticks,
& Sarcoptic
mange

ACTIVE
INGREDIENT:
& (Mecapto-
methyl) phthal
imide) (6.0) 0
(dimethyl phosphoro-
dithioate) 11.60%
INERT INGREDIENTS: 88.40%*
* Contains aromatic petroleum solvent

Protect from temperatures below 20°F

Keep out of reach of children
WARNING
Read all directions and precautions before
using. See side panel for Note to
Physician/Veterinarian

4 FL. OZ. (118 ml)

ZODIAC 🔥
PET PROTECTION PROGRAM

Flea & Tick
Shampoo
FOR DOGS & CATS

Kills fleas & ticks
Adds luster &
groomability
pet's coat

Keep out of reach of children
CAUTION
See back panel for additional caution.

12 FL. OZ. (.35 L)

ZODIAC ~~STEP~~ **2**
PET PROTECTION PROGRAM

11 Month
Flea Collar
FOR DOGS

Kills fleas up to 11 months
Kills ticks up to 7 months

Aids in tick control for an
additional 2 months

Aids in prevention of Sarcoptic
mange up to 5 months

Contains DURSBAN®
ACTIVE INGREDIENT:
Chlorpyrifos, 0,0-diethyl 0-(3,5,6-trichloro-2-pyridyl)
phosphorothioate 4.0%
INERT INGREDIENTS: 96.0%

Keep out of reach of children
CAUTION
See other precautions on back

NET WT. 1.3 OZ. (36.9g)

ZODIAC ~~STEP~~ **4**
PET PROTECTION PROGRAM

Water-Based

Flea & Tick
Pump Spray
For Cats & Dogs

Kills fleas, lice & ticks
Kills roach, gnats, flies,
& mosquitos
Contains Lanolin

ACTIVE INGREDIENTS: Pyrethrins
0.10%, Piperonyl butoxide, technical 1%,
N-Octyl bicycloheptene
dicarboximide 1%, Di-n-propyl
isocinchomeronate 0.50%
INERT INGREDIENTS: 98.917%

CAUTION

16 FL. OZ. (473 ml)

Phase I Concept A

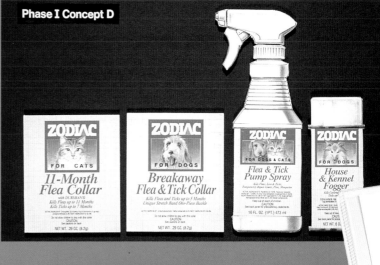

Phase I Concept D

Phase I Concept H

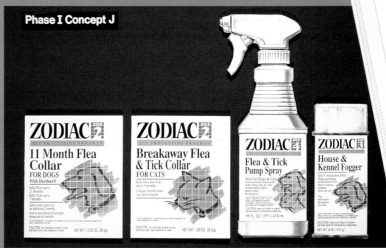

Phase I Concept J

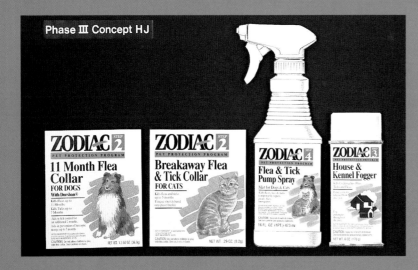

Phase III Concept HJ

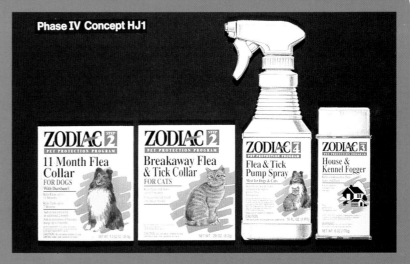

Phase IV Concept HJ1

After additional consideration and refinements, elements from designs H and J were combined in Phase III. This design seemed to best address all of the program's primary objectives.

In Phase IV, the combined design received its final refinements which included some adjustments to sizing, positioning and final color selection. This design became the new Zodiac imagery.

144

During the first phase of the developmental program, a wide variety of logos and images were developed. Alternate ways to picture animals on the package fronts were also explored. From among the ten concepts presented in Phase One, four concepts were selected for further development.

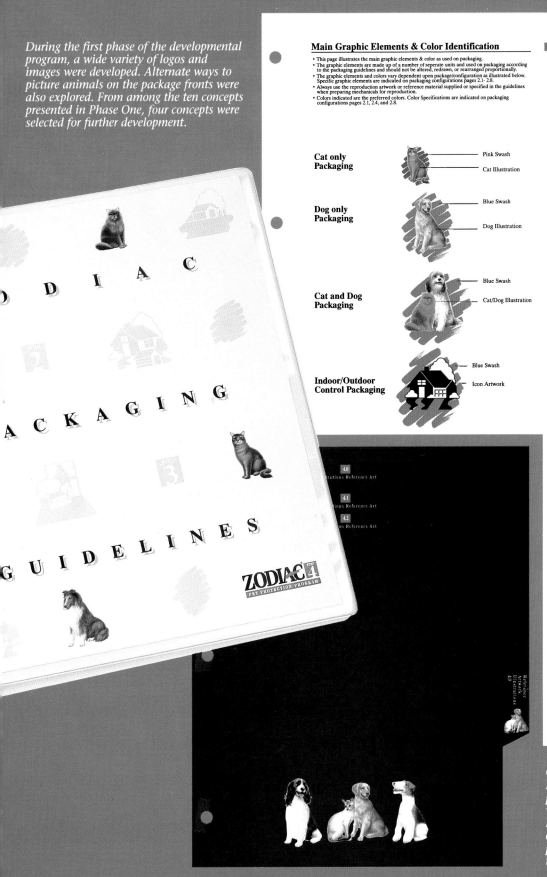

Main Graphic Elements & Color Identification   `1.4`

- This page illustrates the main graphic elements & color as used on packaging.
- The graphic elements are made up of a number of seperate units and used on packaging according to the packaging guidelines and should not be altered, redrawn, or rearranged proportionally.
- The graphic elements and colors vary dependent upon package/configuration as illustrated below. Specific graphic elements are indicated on packaging configurations pages 2.1- 2.8.
- Always use the reproduction artwork or reference material supplied or specified in the guidelines when preparing mechanicals for reproduction.
- Colors indicated are the preferred colors. Color Specifications are indicated on packaging configurations pages 2.1, 2.4, and 2.8.

Cat only Packaging — Pink Swash / Cat Illustration

Dog only Packaging — Blue Swash / Dog Illustration

Cat and Dog Packaging — Blue Swash / Cat/Dog Illustration

Indoor/Outdoor Control Packaging — Blue Swash / Icon Artwork

Package Design Guidelines   `2.1`
Configuration: Small, Narrow (Front Panel) Carton

- Panels shown actual size.
- Other panels (not shown) copy size no smaller than 6pt. Helvetica Condensed and Bold Condensed, depending on amount of copy.
- Follow general layout and proportions as illustrated. Layout may vary depending on amount of copy.
- One rule divides two statements, two rules divide three statements.

Top Panel

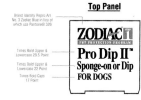

Back Panel   **Front Panel**

CLS&M developed a Packaging Guidelines Manual for use by Zodiac's internal production staffers and outside packaging vendors. The purpose of the Guidelines Manual is to help maintain the integrity of the new design as new products and packages are developed and as the design is translated for international use.

145

The Gillette Company wished to expand its line of hair care products for men, adding new product forms such as aerosol styling mousse. Creating a more contemporary, masculine image with greater shelf impact, while maintaining equity with the existing logotype and color coding, the designers developed a bold graphic symbol which became the focal point for the entire line. The distinctive color code system indicates the various strengths of the products; gray for regular hold, red for extra hold and brown for maximum hold.

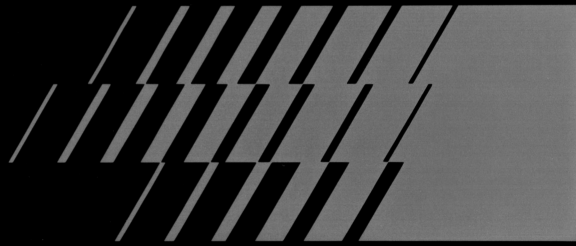

The male portraits on the existing packaging were too easily dated and not dramatic enough to compete in today's hair care category.

Gillette
THE DRY LOOK
EXTRA HOLD
AEROSOL HAIR SPRAY
NET WT. 5 OZ.
Gillette
THE DRY LOOK
REGULAR HOLD
AEROSOL HAIR SPRAY
NET WT. 5 OZ.
Gillette
THE DRY LOOK
MAX HOLD
Gillette
THE DRY LOOK
EXTRA HOLD
Gillette
THE DRY LOOK
REGULAR HOLD
PUMP HAIR SPRAY
Gillette
THE DRY LOOK
EXTRA FULLNESS
STYLING MOUSSE
NET WT. 5 OZ.
Gillette
THE DRY LOOK
REGULAR
STYLING MOUSSE
NET WT. 5 OZ.
Gillette
THE DRY LOOK
STYLING GEL
NET WT. 3.5 OZ.

A strategic decision to upgrade the Magic line of sizing and starch products was made by Dial Marketing Management so that the product line would achieve better recognition in the marketplace. Visually powerful symbols were created to graphically communicate and separate the individual products' usages.

The Magic Sizing logostyle was slightly modified and retained as part of the equity of the exisiting packaging, combined with a strong color coding system.

The existing packaging image had been redesigned about ten years ago and looked dated. Dial Marketing Management wanted a bold, contemporary image that related to a younger consumer.

Initial rough color magic marker concepts were reviewed by the design team prior to positioning each of the proposed package design themes in the computer.

The new packaging projects a contemporary image through the use of all white backgrounds with color-coding for the individual products.

The pet food business has developed into the second largest grocery category in the supermarket, second only to paper goods. A subsegment within the overall pet food business is dog and cat treat products. Treats tend to fall into two general categories; biscuits and other treats (jerky, rawhide, etc.). Historically, James Spratt, an American living in London, started selling the first commercial pet food

in 1860 (it was a hard seaman's biscuit). He opened for business in New York in 1895 and since then, the pet business has come a long way.

CLS&M retained a strong Friskies trademark and developed a premium quality image across 40 Friskies Master's Choice treat products. Diagonal gold lines are a consistent pattern across dog and cat treat products with strong color coding for product differentiation. A black background is used for dog treats and turquoise for cat treats.

Superior Brands, Inc. had a line of pet treats/rawhide chews marketed under the Master's Choice brand name within the pet section of the supermarket trade. The Nestlé Company acquired Superior Brands which resulted in a package design program for a line of dog and cat treats with a view towards expansion into other pet supplies. CLS&M combined the important Friskies brand name with Master's Choice as a sub-brand name in developing a line of 35 dog treat items and five Friskies cat treats.

Several package design themes were created working initially with the dog food biscuits and kitty teasers packaging. Concepts included appealing pet food photography. Several trademark logo formats were established and positioned on design themes.

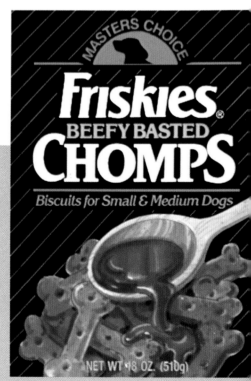

152

Friskies

KITTY NIP

PREMIUM CAT TREATS

GROW AT HOME CATNIP PLANT

*Grows Indoors
Just Add Water*

Contains
EVERYTHING
You Need To Grow
Fresh Kitty Nip
For Your Cat

CONTAINS 1 UNIT
U.S. PATENT NO. 4,124,953

Final packaging utilized full-color illustration of dogs and cats with friendly, animated faces.

Friskies

KITTY TEASERS
PREMIUM CAT TREATS

Beef Flavor

Moist & Tender
POUCH NET WT. 4 OZ. (113g)

Friskies

MASTER'S CHOICE
PREMIUM DOG TREATS

*Beefy Basted
Chomps*

Biscuits for Small & Medium Dogs
NET WT 18 OZ. (510g)

KITTY TEASERS

Friskies

PREMIUM CAT TREATS

Beef Flavor

Moist & Tender
CONTAINS 1 POUCH NET WT 4 OZ. (113g)

MASTER'S CHOICE

Friskies

PREMIUM DOG TREATS

*Beefy Basted
Chomps*

Biscuits For
Small & Medium Dogs
NET WT 18 OZ. (510g)

Critical to the selection of CLS&M's favored design candidate theme was the positioning of each design in a multiple computer planogram format, positioned next to competitive products. Planogram "B" was selected for the black dog treat packaging, and Planogram "A" for the cat treat packaging in turquoise.

A

The old Master's Choice packaging (left) was bold, but lacked a quality image. The new chomps packaging (above) combined appetite appeal and a strong quality impression.

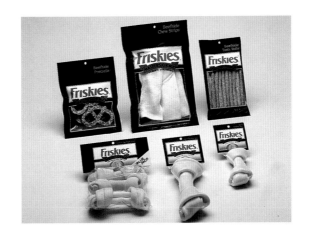

The new packaging has been extremely well received by the trade and sales have shown a marked increase.

B

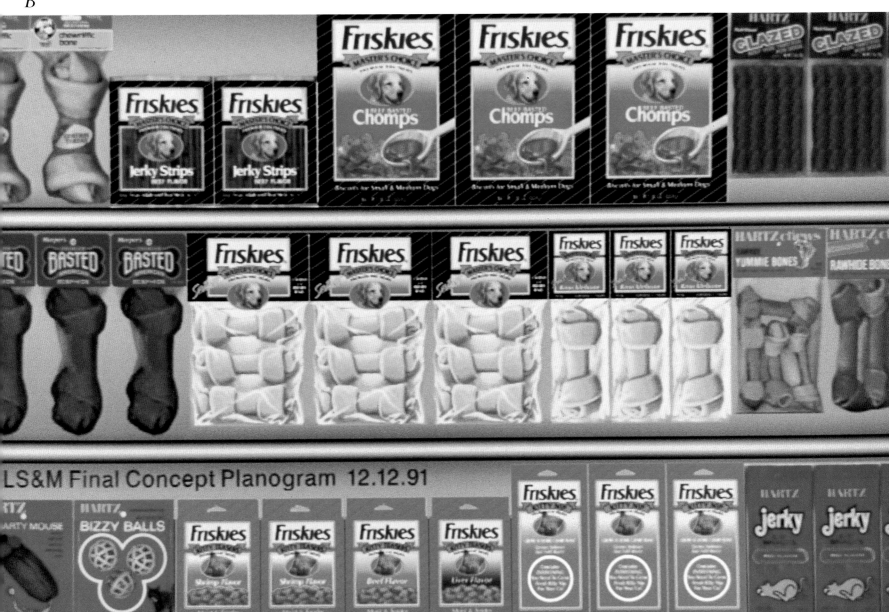

CORELLE®
IMPRESSIONS™

DINNERWARE BY **CORNING**

A fresh, upscale image was required for the new line of elegantly-embossed Corelle dinnerware products by Corning. A unique logotype/brand image was created for this new Impressions segment, linking it to the existing Corelle logotype. The overall image adds a fashionable, contemporary dimension to Corelle's "best" dinnerware segment.

High-quality photography positions the dinnerware within a graceful airbrushed swirl background which accentuates the sculptured product styling.

157

In 1966 the design company was founded and, in a short time, solid business relationships with many corporations were established. From the beginning our specialization was packaging design which encompassed three-dimensional structure for glass, plastics and boxboard with applied graphics.

Over a decade ago, Owen W. Coleman, President of CLS&M, pioneered in the introduction of computer-aided design for packaging in the United States & Europe. We were working on the redesign of the Nestea beverage line and Nestlé marketing Vice President, Hank McInerney, showed us a video tape of a major design study on the same subject matter executed with a technique developed by Nestlé Design Management in Vevey, Switzerland called Videography. To our amazement, every five seconds a package design of the Nestea label appeared on the video screen in full color form.

Within another year, several independent companies began to produce graphic computers that could be used to create advertising materials or packaging. The first of these systems that gained some popularity was the Via Video System. Within a short period of time we became aware of the Lightspeed Design System 10, Contex systems, Aesthedes and Unda Systems. It was an exciting time visualizing the potential of design created on a video screen. During those years very few of us thought that the little Apple Macintosh would become the winner of the hardware wars.

The impulse was to run out and acquire the equipment as quickly as possible. In retrospect, it made great sense not to do that, but to experiment with the new technology at the manufacturers offices or at an access studio. Of course, everyone was looking for the magic computer equipment on which you could create a package design and with a click of the mouse produce an electronic mechanical for reproduction.

We explored the computer potential for packaging design in 1984 with several clients and found a true pioneering spirit with four people—Tony Parisi, Director of Design at General Foods, Maurice Joseph, Design Director at Nabisco Brands, Bill Maginnis, Director of Design at Beatrice /Hunt-Wesson and Max Lomont, Vice President of Design at the Quaker Oats Company. Fortunately for us, these four important accounts recognized the long-range potential of the electronics medium and supported our design organization during the experimental stages with computers.

During that time, we were working on a major upgrade program for a Quaker Oats Company/Aunt Jemima brand redesign program at Lightspeed Systems access studio in Boston and at G.S. Imaging in New Jersey for a full week averaging 16-hour days. We were novices at that point in time and neglected to save the steps in the computer design process along the way. Quaker was expecting a presentation on Monday afternoon and on Saturday at 1 a.m. the job was completed and suddenly the machine went berserk! All the new package designs were flashing before us and disappearing somewhere under the computer table into a myriad of connections and wires we knew nothing about. We were concerned that this "electronic stuff" could put us out of business. Fortunately, we were working with G.S. Imaging who had several computer whiz kids on staff. On Sunday morning they arrived and, within three hours, retrieved the electronic design images that were miraculously saved somewhere in storage. We converted all the digitized information to full-color 35mm slides and made our first major computer design presentation to the Quaker Oats Company in Chicago. We made sure the clients' strategic design objectives were resolved and because the Lightspeed computer system allowed us to experiment easily, we showed Quaker a major package design change different from their original criteria.

The most critical slide within the entire presentation was the computer planogram. By changing the background of the package color, the multiple packaging images created an immediate blocking effect within the competitive clutter. The Quaker Divisional President was urgently called out of a meeting to look at this slide and a critical strategic marketing decision

Initial Lightspeed & Macintosh concept package design.   *Output as color laser prints for staff & client review.*   *The first remote design presentation to the U.K.--1987.*

was made to make a more revolutionary change in the packaging design. To our knowledge, we had created the first major computer packaging planogram and the reaction was extraordinary. This was a high point in our package design presentation and it dwarfed the disasters of the previous week.

Like many design organizations, we were hesitant to make major capital investments in equipment. Ours was a people/talent business which did not require machinery that might become obsolete in a year or less. Computer companies were popping up all over the place.

A few years ago it was difficult to keep up with the computer systems companies. Now it's virtually impossible to keep up with all the graphics software available for packaging design on the Mac Quadra. We also recognized the potential of remote viewing. The Optel Remote Viewing System is linked to our Lightspeed unit and we successfully initiated experiments with some of our Midwest clients, 3M, Pillsbury, and General Mills.

On a recent redesign program for Findus Frozen Foods in Croydon, U.K., the Senior Brand Manager, Frank McKeown and CLS&M Europe Managing Partner, Steve Merry, were reviewing a full-color package design concept with us in New York on the U.K. remote viewing system when the General Manager of Findus Frozen Foods, Richard Webb, walked by and pondered the video image. "What would the Findus logo look like," he asked, "in relation to the rest of the pack if it was positioned lower as a signature?" Fifteen minutes later we transmitted the revised image from New York to the United Kingdom for his review. Additional design suggestions were annotated in "real time" on the video screen as we communicated on the telephone. Having the capability to make transatlantic design changes like that was virtually unthinkable only a few years ago.

Based on the positive reaction we were getting from design management around the country, we started our first CLS&M computer design seminar in 1985 and gathered twenty-two of the leading design management executives together at a full-day meeting. The Techtron/Wace Group of companies became our co-sponsor for these seminars. We have since had five exciting seminars with hundreds of our colleagues which have now extended to four-day sessions in various locations throughout the United States. This packaging seminar has now changed its focus from computer equipment and software to output devices and managing the systems with total electronic communication, fulfilling global marketing strategies.

The excitement and the pioneering spirit is still there, but some of the hype and show biz quality has diminished. Industrial design firms are now involved in major capital expenditures for computers, training programs and continuous equipment upgrades. But it's still a people/talent business which is critical to the success or failure of all of us.

Despite the hype, we have always maintained that design excellence is the critical factor and our main selling point. The electronic tools have proven most beneficial to the client. Last year we designed and prepared over 480 packaging SKU's electronically. We are now remoting creative design and electronic mechanicals to our clients throughout the United States and abroad and to our design office, CLS&M Europe, based in London. We are part of a revolution that has totally changed the design industry.

When Coleman, LiPuma, Segal & Morrill started, none of us could have predicted the power of the brand image and the impact of computers for strategic development of a total communications package for our clients worldwide.

Owen W. Coleman, Sal LiPuma, Abe Segal, & Ed Morrill personally wish to acknowledge the extraordinary efforts of the many people who, through the years, have devoted themselves to our design organization on behalf of our clients:

Larry Aaron	*Ed Kozloski*
James Ahern	*William Lee*
Leon Ajemian	*Tom Li*
Sarah Allen	*Vitatherese LoFria*
Ellen Avella	*Susan Mandel*
Chava Ben-Amos	*Camille Maravegias*
Walter Blugerman	*Bernie Marks*
Rickey Bradley	*Patricia Martin*
Randy Brown	*Marvin Maslow*
Efren Canlas	*Steve Merry*
Robert Chapman	*Wayne Molinare*
J.C. Chou	*Joan Nicosia*
John Chrzanowski	*Chris Papadakis*
Karen Corell	*Richard Roth*
Oscar Dubrow	*John Rutig*
Connie Fenton	*Emmit Sears*
Eileen Ferara	*Shelley Seif*
Lorraine Fierro	*Patricia Slade*
Joyce Forrester	*Anne Swan*
Ladd Fraternale	*Catherine SzeTu*
Steve Fuchs	*Thaddeus Szumilas*
Sue Geramian	*Peter Thompson*
Marilyn Goodacre	*Joe Trainor*
Greg Hodgman	*Marianne Walther*
Ward Hooper	*Paula Welch*
Harvey Hunerberg	*Carol Winer*
Adrian Johnson	*Simon Wong*

A special thanks to all the wonderful clients we have had the privilege to work with over the years.

For many of us, our closest personal friendships have been built with people in the corporate and graphic arts communities.

Now that we have embraced the new electronic technologies, the next five years may prove to be the most challenging as we focus on the globalization of brands.

CLS&M's Littlest Intern

Coleman, LiPuma, Segal & Morrill, Inc., noted international industrial design firm, became the proud surrogate parents to Ryan Fries, born on October 9, 1991. Ryan's mother wished to return to work soon after his birth to insure the smooth running of the design firm's accounting department. While searching for reliable child care, a temporary nursery was set up in her office. At first, management was concerned with the possible disruption a newborn might cause in a busy design office. Fears that Ryan would disturb meetings and distract staffers were soon allayed, as he conducted himself most professionally in all situations. It was not uncommon to find Ryan at staff meetings, photo shoots and on the laps of various members of the organization, where he gained broad exposure to word processing, accounting procedures and the capabilities of computer-aided packaging design. His sunny, magnetic personality captivated even the most stoic of the group, and the search for childcare was postponed for ten months. He has recently been promoted to a daycare center where he will begin networking with shorter people.

NEW YORK: *Coleman, LiPuma, Segal & Morrill, Inc., 305 East 46th Street, New York, NY 10017* • Telephone 212/421-9030 • Fax 212/755-5238
LONDON: *Coleman, LiPuma, Segal & Morrill Europe, Shepherdess Walk, London N1 7LH* • Telephone 071/490-3115 • Fax 071/490-4916